SOUTHWARK'S BURYING PLACES

~ PAST & PRESENT ~

A guide to the parish churchyards,
nonconformist graveyards, private burial grounds, and cemeteries
in the London Borough of Southwark.

by RON WOOLLACOTT

A 'MAGDALA TERRACE NUNHEAD'
Local History Publication
MMI

Acknowledgments

I am indebted to Mr Terry Connor M.Inst.BCA, Superintendent and Registrar of Southwark Cemeteries, and to his predecessors Messrs Arthur Vercouttere, Lou Hedger and Jeff Webber, for their help and co-operation in allowing me to study various documents and burial records relating to the now defunct London Cemetery Company and Burial Board of St Giles, Camberwell.

I should like to thank the staff of Southwark Local Studies Library, in particular former local studies librarians Miss Mary Boast and Ms Nicola Smith who were most helpful when I began researching the subject of Southwark's former burial grounds, and Southwark archivist Mr Stephen Humphrey for his helpful advice. Thanks also to local historian John D Beasley for providing a copy of the site plan of the former Wesleyan Chapel Burial Ground in Peckham.

I am especially grateful to my wife Maureen and to her sister Miss Linda Martin for accompanying me on numerous expeditions throughout the London Borough of Southwark in search of former burial grounds.

Finally, I should like to thank my daughter Mrs Michele Louise Burford for reading the manuscript and for offering helpful suggestions.

Introduction

Until the founding of the great Metropolitan cemeteries in the second quarter of the 19th century, London's dead were buried in parish churches and churchyards - many of which had been in use for many centuries - or else in one of the numerous Dissenters' or privately run burying grounds that were situated in and around the capital.

The deplorable state of London's overcrowded and disease-ridden graveyards led to the formation of joint-stock cemetery companies and to the establishment of spacious profit-making cemeteries situated outside the built-up area, the first of which was opened at Kensal Green by the General Cemetery Company in 1833.

Nunhead Cemetery was the first public cemetery established in what is now the London Borough of Southwark. Founded by the London Cemetery Company in 1840, it provided burial facilities to anyone who could afford it; in catacombs, vaults, private graves and common plots. Consequently, people from all over the Greater London area and further afield were buried there.

Despite the opening of the new cemeteries most of Southwark's dead, as indeed most of London's dead, continued to be buried in insanitary churchyards and crowded graveyards, until the campaign to close all the London burial grounds led by George Alfred Walker, a surgeon, bath-house proprietor and zealous burial reformer, prompted the Government into taking action.

The 1852 Burial Act (15 & 16 Vic. Ch. 85), one of several Burial Acts passed in the 1850s, empowered the Metropolitan Parish Authorities to appoint Burial Boards and to establish cemeteries of their own. This was followed in 1853 by the Burial Act [16 & 17 Vic. Ch. 134] and under Sections 1 and 3 of this particular Act a large number of burying grounds in the London area were permanently closed, including 35 churchyards and burial grounds in what is now the London Borough of Southwark.*

The Parish of St Giles' Camberwell opened a cemetery at Honor Oak, but its poorer and more densely populated neighbours, including the Parishes of St Saviour, St George the Martyr and Christ Church, Southwark, and the Parishes in Rotherhithe and Bermondsey, elected to make use of the privately-owned public cemeteries such as those at Nunhead and Brookwood.

The fate of the closed and abandoned graveyards has been well documented by Mrs Basil Holmes (*The London Burial Grounds* 1896); some were built upon while others became rubbish dumping grounds.

In 1882 the Metropolitan Public Gardens Association was established, and two years later the Disused Burial Grounds Act came into force prohibiting building on former burial grounds. By 1900 at least 18 former graveyards throughout the Southwark area had been converted into much needed public gardens or recreation grounds.

Nowadays old burial grounds are no longer protected from the developers. The Disused Burial Grounds (Amendment) Act of 1981 permits building on former graveyards (other than Church of England sites which require a Bishop's Faculty) provided that all human remains are treated with respect, carefully removed and cremated or re-buried elsewhere.

On the following pages I have attempted to list all those burying places in Southwark that I have been able to identify from various sources, including old plans, maps and books, and from Mrs Holmes invaluable list. Some graveyards were known by more than one name at different times, and where possible I have included the alternative name as a separate entry. Old style addresses are followed by the nearest modern equivalent (in parentheses). Burying places marked with an asterisk either no longer exist or identification of the actual site has not been possible.

Some grounds may be included more than once under different names. For example, I have been unable to establish whether Hoole & Martins Burial Ground, Newington and Martin's Burial Ground, Borough is one and the same. I have therefore included them as separate entries.

Today there are just three burying places in the London Borough of Southwark; all three are large cemeteries located in the south of the borough (the former Metropolitan Borough of Camberwell) with limited space for future burials. Honor Oak Crematorium, also in the south of the borough was opened in 1939, and cremation now accounts for the disposal of around 79% of all Southwark's deceased citizens.

* Includes the districts of Bermondsey, the Borough, Camberwell, Dulwich, Newington, Peckham, Walworth and Rotherhithe.

Note. The figures in italics at the end of each entry refer to the sources, a list of which will be found on page 29.

AGED PILGRIMS ASYLUM, CAMBERWELL
Westmoreland Place, Camberwell, Surrey
(Sedgmoor Place, London, SE5)
The Aged Pilgrims' Friendly Society was founded in 1807. In 1837 almshouses were built in Westmoreland Place, near Southampton Street (now Southampton Way) on land given by William Peacock. Mr Peacock died in 1844 and his remains were interred in a special vault in the courtyard. *23; 57*

ALL SAINTS' CHURCHYARD, ROTHERHITHE
Deptford Lower Road, Rotherhithe, Surrey
(Lower Road, London, SE16)
All Saints' Church was built in 1840 to the designs of Sampson Kempthorne (1809-73) on land given to the parish by Field Marshal Sir William Maynard Gomm, Lord of the Manor. The churchyard was in use from 1843 to 1857, although the last recorded burial was in 1888.

The church was bombed during World War II. In 1952 the Parish of All Saints' was united with St Mary Rotherhithe (qv). A small garden called King George's Fields was built on the site. *10; 24; 34; 43; 44; 58*

BACK STREET CHAPEL BURIAL GROUND, BERMONDSEY
(see NECKINGER ROAD CHAPEL BURIAL GROUND)

BANDYLEG WALK BURIAL GROUND, SOUTHWARK*
Bandyleg Walk, Southwark, Surrey
(Great Guildford Street, London, SE1)
This small burial ground was opened by Southwark Baptists about 1729. It probably adjoined St Saviour's Workhouse burial ground for paupers *(see New Grotto Burial Ground)*. It was afterwards used as a private garden until 1878 when it was acquired by the Metropolitan Board of Works for the site of a fire station.

In May 1988, while laying drainage pipes in the car park (part of the former burial ground) next to the Fire Brigade Training Centre, workmen uncovered numerous skeletons just four feet below the surface of the ground. The human remains were removed to a cemetery in East London. *20; 43*

BERMONDSEY ABBEY BURIAL GROUND*
Bermondsey, Surrey
(Bermondsey Market, London, SE1)
Bermondsey Abbey was founded in 1082 by Aylwin Child, a wealthy London merchant, and dedicated to St Saviour. The first monks, belonging to the Cluniac order, a branch of Benedictines, arrived in Bermondsey in 1089.

In 1537 the Abbey was surrendered to Henry VIII and pulled down soon after. Within five years Thomas Pope had erected Bermondsey House on the site using material salvaged from the demolished buildings.

The Abbey burial ground was incorporated with that of St Mary Magdalen (qv), and during reconstruction work a stone coffin was discovered. Several more ancient graves were uncovered by workmen in the 1950s. In recent years further discoveries have been made.

Loufstone, Provost or Domesman of London, was buried here in 1115, and Thomas, Duke of Gloucester, was temporarily buried here in 1387. His remains were later removed to Westminster Abbey. *43; 55; 30*

BERMONDSEY CHURCHYARD
(see ST MARY MAGDALEN, BERMONDSEY)

BERMONDSEY ROMAN CATHOLIC BURIAL GROUND*
Dockhead, Bermondsey, Surrey
(Parkers Row, London, SE1)
The Roman Catholic Church of the Most Holy Trinity was built in 1835. Pugin's Convent of the Sisters of Mercy adjoined the church. The churchyard and gardens of both buildings were used for burials until about 1853. The grounds were later used for recreational purposes.

The church and the convent were both destroyed by enemy action during World War II. A new church was built on the site in 1960. *34; 43; 57*

BROOKWOOD CEMETERY, WOKING, SURREY
Brookwood Cemetery was opened by the London Necropolis Company in November 1854 to provide burial facilities for the whole of London and its suburbs, including Southwark. Over 400 acres were set aside for burial purposes with many more held in reserve. Mr Donald of Woking, the Company's landscape gardener, laid out 'future avenues, terraces, lawns, grassy knolls, and fringing belts of woodland with admirable effect'. He also planted magnolias, azaleas and rhododendrons amongst the 'American evergreens'.

A railway station was built at Westminster Bridge Road and special trains carried coffins and mourners direct to stations situated within the cemetery.

A great number of Southwark's dead were buried in Brookwood's beautiful grounds. Indeed, the first three burials were from the Borough. The Burial Board of the Parish of St Saviour was one of the first burial authorities to enter into a contract with Brookwood Cemetery, thus in 1853 over 6 acres of burial land were set aside for the exclusive use of that parish.

In 1895, the remains of 650 persons were interred at Brookwood having been removed from the vaults under Christ Church, Blackfriars Road (qv). Four years later the crypt of St George the Martyr, Borough (qv) was cleared and 1,500 coffins were buried in a special plot at Brookwood. The site of the mass grave was marked by a replica (now collapsed) of the obelisk that stands in St George's Circus, Southwark. *11; 16; 27; 37; 55*

BUTLER'S BURIAL GROUND, HORSELYDOWN*
Coxon's Place, later 22 Butler's Place, Horselydown
(near Fair Street, SE1)
This was a private speculation opened by a local undertaker about 1822. Having obtained some land for burial purposes, the undertaker later acquired the cellars under four houses adjoining the ground and converted them into burial vaults. An assistant masqueraded as a Minister of Religion at funerals.

This grossly overcrowded burial ground was closed in the 1850s and was afterwards used as a cooperage by Edmund Zurhorst. Mr Zurhorst died in 1865 and was buried in Nunhead Cemetery. As late as 1894 Mrs Holmes noted that the cellars beneath the houses still existed, and were packed with coffins. *43; 51*

CAMBERWELL CEMETERY
Wood Lane, Peckham Rye, Camberwell, Surrey
(Forest Hill Road, London, SE22)

Camberwell Cemetery was one of five cemeteries established within the boundary of the future County of London between the years 1854 and 1856 under the 'Burials (Beyond the Limits of the Metropolis) Act, 15 and 16 Vic. c.85, and other Acts incorporated therewith.'

Camberwell Cemetery, or to give its full title, *The Burial Ground of Saint Giles' Parish in the County of Surrey, situate at Forest Hill, Peckham Rye, Surrey*, was owned by the local authority (the Vestry of the Parish of St Giles, Camberwell) and managed by a Burial Board of elected rate-payers. The cemetery, with buildings designed by Sir George Gilbert Scott, was opened in July 1856. Within 18 years over 30,000 bodies had been interred in the 31 acre site, consequently in 1874 the cemetery was enlarged by the addition of another seven acres. The land was quickly used up and graves were dug in the cemetery's pathways and roadways.

In 1927 the Borough of Camberwell opened a new cemetery nearby, but the older cemetery, renamed Camberwell Old Cemetery, continued to be used where families owned space in private graves and vaults. The Anglican and Nonconformist chapels were bomb damaged and demolished in the 1940s, and the Roman Catholic chapel was demolished in the 1970s. Many memorials were cleared away and broken up in the 1960s and 1970s. By 1984 over 300,000 bodies had been buried here.

Many Camberwell notables lie buried here including: William Harnett Blanch (d.1900), author of *Ye Parish of Cam(b)erwell*; Admiral Andrew Drew RN (d.1878); Edward Wilmot Seale (d.1867), proprietor of the Sunday Times; Camilla Dufour Toulmin (d.1895) novelist; and James Waterlow (d.1876), founder of Waterlow & Sons, printers and stationers. Several interesting monuments still exist including the tombs of James Berkley (d.1862) railway engineer; Robert Alexander Gray (d.1877) known as the 'Father of Camberwell' and Frederick Horniman (d.1906) the founder of Horniman's Museum. The Berkley and Horniman monuments are Listed Grade II by English Heritage.

In 1965 the Boroughs of Camberwell, Bermondsey and Southwark were amalgamated and the ownership of Camberwell Old Cemetery passed to the newly constituted London Borough of Southwark. *01; 09; 23; 43; 50; 62*

CAMBERWELL CHURCHYARD
(see ST GILES' CHURCH, CAMBERWELL)

CAMBERWELL NEW CEMETERY, HONOR OAK
(Brenchley Gardens, London, SE23)

This cemetery was established under the 'Burials (Beyond the Metropolis) Acts 15 & 16 Victoria c.85' on land acquired by the Metropolitan Borough of Camberwell in 1901. The cemetery was built to supplement Camberwell Cemetery (qv), and was originally called *The New Cemetery Burial Ground of the Borough of Camberwell in the County of London situated at Honor Oak*. The name was later shortened to Camberwell New Cemetery, but is often referred to as Honor Oak Cemetery by local people.

The central portion of the cemetery ground (about 24 acres) was purchased from Alfred Stevens of Peckham Rye in June 1901 for the sum of £11,305. The western portion adjoining One Tree Hill (32 acres) was bought of the same landowner at the same time for £19,469. In November 1901 another plot of land (12 acres) adjoining the footpath to Brockley (now Brockley Way) was purchased from the Governors of Christ's Hospital for £6,325. The greater part of the site, not being immediately required for burial purposes, was let on a ten-year lease from 1909 to 1919 to the Honor Oak Golf Club. A small plot at Honor Oak Park was let on a quarterly tenancy to James Wells, the pyrotechnist, for the site of a fireworks factory.

On Saturday 30th April 1927, during the mayoralty of Councillor Herbert William Shalders, part of the site was consecrated by the Rt Revd William Woodcock Hough, Lord Bishop of Woolwich, and the first burials took place on Friday 23rd May 1927. The General Section was dedicated by Free Church Ministers on Friday 24th June 1927. The twin chapels were designed by Sir Aston Webb.

By 1982 the cemetery was almost full, although much of the land originally acquired for burial purposes continued to be used as a recreation ground. Despite vociferous protests from users and residents, a portion of the recreation ground was set aside for future burials. It has now been brought into use.

Freddie Mills, the British boxer, and Light Heavyweight Champion of the World 1948-50, was laid to rest here in 1965. Other persons of note buried here include Johnny Trunley (d.1944), heavyweight actor, known as 'The Fat Boy of Peckham'; Bertram Gallanaugh (d.1957), City of London architect; Arthur Bateman (d.1957) MP for North Camberwell and former Mayor of Camberwell; William Pullum (d.1960), bodybuilder and World Weight-lifting Champion; and Anne Shelton OBE (d.1994), popular vocalist, known as the "Forces' Favourite" during World War II. A small enclosed plot contains the graves of officers of the Salvation Army including that of General Wilfred Kitching (d.1977).

In 1965 the Metropolitan Borough of Camberwell was amalgamated with the Boroughs of Bermondsey and Southwark and since then the cemetery has been managed by the London Borough of Southwark. It is well maintained. *08; 28; 50; 53*

CAMBERWELL OLD CEMETERY
(see CAMBERWELL CEMETERY)

CHAPEL GRAVEYARD, COLLIERS RENTS*
Colliers Rents, Long Lane, Southwark, Surrey
(Tennis Street, London, SE1)

This small burying ground adjoined a Baptist chapel which opened about 1700. Many gravestones existed in the late 1890s, even though burials had not taken place for many years. The burial ground was converted into a public garden at the cost of the Congregational Union, and opened on the 18th June 1900. It was obliterated by bombing during World War II. *27; 31; 43*

page 7

Remains of tombstones and commemorative stone in the churchyard of
Christ Church, Blackfriars Road, Southwark. (Photograph of 1989 by the author). *See page 8.*

A view of the modern Christ Church, Southwark from Colombo Street.
The site of the additional burial ground is in the foreground. (Photograph of 1989 by the author). *See page 8.*

CHRIST CHURCH, SOUTHWARK
Great Surrey Street, Southwark, Surrey
(Blackfriars Road, London, SE1)

Christ Church, Southwark was only partially built when it was consecrated in 1671. It was eventually completed in 1695. The vaults beneath the chancel were built by William Angell, the Lord of the Manor, and were reserved for the interment of the builder and his heirs.

The church stood on former marshland and as a consequence the vaults and graves were often flooded.

In 1741 Christ Church was rebuilt and the graveyard extended. In 1817 several cottages adjoining the church were demolished and the graveyard was again enlarged. The first burial took place in 1671 and the last in 1856.

In 1895 several lead coffins in the crypt were found to be seriously damaged by heat from the boilers, while others were found lying in water. Mr J. D. Field, a member of the church and the local undertaker, was contracted to remove over 650 bodies from the church vaults and during the months of April and May the coffins were transferred to a special plot in Brookwood Cemetery (qv).

In June 1900 the churchyard was dedicated to the public by the Bishop of Rochester. The grounds were laid out as a park at the expense of the Metropolitan Public Gardens Association, and St Saviour's District Board of Works took over the maintenance. A drinking fountain, the gift of J. Pasmore Edwards, was erected in the centre of the new garden.

Christ Church was bombed in April 1941 and many registers were either severely damaged or else destroyed. A new church was built on the same site in 1960.

In 1990 a few tombs remained in the public garden and several gravestones formed a pavement around the church walls. A flat stone commemorates Captain Thomas Eyre Hinton RN (d.1829), and another commemorates John Lloyd Esquire (d.1836), millwright and engineer. *10; 27; 43; 55; 57; 58*

CHRIST CHURCH, SOUTHWARK (ADDITIONAL BURIAL GROUND)
Collingwood Street, Southwark, Surrey
(Colombo Street, London, SE1)

This burial ground was laid out in 1816 to supplement the existing overcrowded parish churchyard and was enclosed to prevent further damage by 'people, swine and dogs'. Burials ceased in 1856 and the ground was laid out as a garden along with the main churchyard in June 1900. The watchhouse, built in 1819 to deter bodysnatchers, was demolished in 1932. *55; 58*

CHRIST CHURCH CHURCHYARD, ROTHERHITHE*
Union Road, Rotherhithe, Surrey
(Jamaica Road/Cathay Street, London, SE1)

Christ Church, Rotherhithe was built in 1840 to the designs of Lewis Vulliamy (1791-1871), and was consecrated in 1842. Burials in the churchyard appear to have commenced in 1840.

In 1875 the body of Field Marshal Sir William Maynard Gomm, Lord of the Manor of Rotherhithe, was interred in the churchyard by special authority. The last interment was that of Lady Gomm in 1877.

In 1950 Christ Church was united with St Crispin, Southwark Park Road. The disused church was demolished as recently as 1979 to make way for road widening improvements. The lead coffins containing the remains of Sir William and Lady Gomm were re-interred at Nunhead Cemetery (qv) in December 1979. The remains of eleven unidentified adults and four children were also exhumed from the churchyard and were re-buried at Nunhead on the 3rd January 1980. *02; 10; 34; 43; 44; 53; 58; 63*

CHRIST'S CHAPEL OF ALLEYN'S COLLEGE OF GOD'S GIFT DULWICH
(see DULWICH COLLEGE CHAPEL)

COLLEGE YARD BURIAL GROUND, SOUTHWARK*
Park Street, Southwark, Surrey
(Borough, London, SE1)

College Yard or St Saviour's Almshouse Burying Ground was opened about 1730 next to almshouses founded by Thomas Cure. In the early 1860s the Charing Cross Railway Company purchased the ground and railway arches were built over it. Part of the ground was roofed over and used by a builders' merchant.

In 1862 the burial ground was cleared and most of the human remains were removed to Brookwood Cemetery, Woking (qv), including the remains of James Dawson (d.1848) late of the George Inn, Borough High Street. Some remains, including the bodies of Ann and Victor Hame of the Borough Market, were exhumed and re-buried at Nunhead Cemetery (qv) on the 14th July 1862. *02; 11; 43*

COLLIERS RENTS BURIAL GROUND, BOROUGH*
White Street, Borough, Surrey
(near Tabard Street, London, SE1)

This small burial ground adjoined a Baptist chapel commenced by the Revd Benjamin Keach. The fellowship was dissolved about 230 years ago.

The burial ground which was 'dotted with the green graves of former members' was afterwards incorporated into the grounds of a brewery. According to Godfrey Pike both the chapel and the graveyard had disappeared by 1870. *54*

CROSS BONES BURIAL GROUND, BOROUGH*
Redcross Street, Borough, Surrey
(Redcross Way/Union Street, London, SE1)

This burial ground, located some distance from the Parish Church of St Saviour, was left unconsecrated to receive the bodies of women from the Bankside brothels or stews, and was also known as the 'Single Women's Graveyard'. From about 1650 the graveyard was used as a burial ground for paupers.

By the early 1800s the burial ground was indecently overcrowded and there were reports of human bones protruding from the earth. In 1849 the inhabitants of Union Street and Redcross Street described the graveyard as an 'outrageous nuisance'. It was finally closed by order

The tomb of Richard Shaw of Casino House in Dulwich Burial Ground.
(Photograph of 1989 by the author). *See page 10.*

The Mausoleum at Dulwich. (Photograph of 1989 by the author). *See page 10.*

of the parish authorities in October 1853. St Saviour's Charity School was built on part of the site and the remaining portion was leased to a showman. St Saviour's Parochial Schools later covered the entire site.

In his *Handbook of London* published 1850, Peter Cunningham claims that the houses in Doddington Grove, Kennington, were built on earth removed from Cross Bones Burial Ground in Southwark.

A quantity of human remains found during building work in the 1920s were taken to Brookwood Cemetery (qv) for re-burial. *11; 26; 43; 55; 57*

CURE'S COLLEGE BURIAL GROUND, BOROUGH
(see COLLEGE YARD BURIAL GROUND).

DEADMAN'S PLACE BURIAL GROUND, BOROUGH*
Deadman's Place, Southwark, Surrey
(Park Street, London SE1)
There was a burial ground here in the reign of Queen Elizabeth I, reputedly the burying place of plague victims. In 1640 it became a burying ground for Dissenters with an Independent chapel in the centre. On Rocque's plan of 1747 the graveyard adjoined a stonecutters yard and tenter ground. It remained in use until about 1837 when Messrs Barclay and Perkins took it over for the site of their brewery. In 1870 Godfrey Pike, the author of *The Metropolitan Tabernacle* wrote: 'Fifty years ago this cemetery remained intact. It has since disappeared'.

Several Dissenting worthies were buried here including the Revd Benjamin Keach (d.1704), evangelist and controversialist; his son-in-law the Revd Benjamin Stinton (d.1718); the Revd John Noble (d.1730), of Maidenhead Court, Great Eastcheap; and Alexander Cruden (d.1770), censor of public morals known as 'Alexander the Corrector' and author of the *Biblical Concordance*. A list of burials dating from 1716 to 1837 was deposited in the Public Record Office. *40; 43; 54; 55; 58; 61*

DENMARK ROW BAPTIST CHAPEL GROUND*
Coldharbour Lane, Camberwell, Surrey
(Coldharbour Lane, London, SE5)
Denmark Row Baptist Chapel was built in 1802 on a triangular plot of land at the junction of Coldharbour Lane and Denmark Hill. The Revd Jonathan Carr was the first Pastor. In 1825 the church was reconstituted and a new place of worship was built called Denmark Place Baptist Church.

By 1895 the burial ground had been built upon leaving a small yard behind the chapel.

The church is situated in the London Borough of Lambeth. *39;43*

DIPPING ALLEY BURIAL GROUND, HORSELYDOWN*
Fair Street, Horselydown, Surrey
(Charles Street/Fair Street, London, SE1)
This burial ground adjoined a meeting house called the 'Baptisterion'. In the seventeenth century, the chapel with dressing rooms attached, was the communal baptising place for those parts of Surrey and Kent which now form South East London. The chapel was reached by way of Dipping Alley, a narrow passage in Fair Street. By the early 1800s it was a preaching station.

Both the chapel and the burial ground have long since disappeared. *43; 54; 58*

DUKE STREET PARK CHAPEL GROUND*
Duke Street Park, Southwark, Surrey
(Duke Street Hill, London, SE1)
A Baptist church was founded in Duke Street Park around 1700. In 1800 the chapel was seized by the heir-at-law and the congregation removed to Gravel Lane. The old chapel and adjoining graveyard were levelled and a hatter's factory was built upon the site. During the clearance work a large family tomb belonging to Captain Pierce Johns was destroyed. *54*

DULWICH BURIAL GROUND
High Street, Dulwich, Camberwell, Surrey
(Court Lane/Dulwich Village, London, SE21)
This tiny burial ground was consecrated by Archbishop Abbott on the 1st September 1616 to receive the bodies of those persons who died in and around the hamlet of Dulwich. It was twice enlarged.

In 1666 thirty-five plague victims were buried here including Nicholas Weekes the local miller. Others of note buried here include Anthony Boheme (d.1731), the famous tragedian; Old Bridgett (d.1768), Queen of the Gypsies; Thomas Jones (d.1807), mathematician; Richard Shaw (d.1816), solicitor to Warren Hastings; and John Horsburgh (d.1836), hydrographer to the Honourable East India Company.

Dulwich Burial Ground was officially closed for burials in 1856, however, in 1898 the Secretary of State gave special permission for Mrs Goodman of the Crown and Greyhound pub in Dulwich Village to be buried here.

The burial ground is cared for and contains several fine monuments. Some headstones have been laid flat. The monument to Richard Shaw of Casino (or Casina) House is signed 'Day of Camberwell'. *23; 36; 42; 43*

DULWICH COLLEGE CHAPEL
Dulwich, Camberwell, Surrey
(College Road, London, SE21)
Dulwich College Chapel was consecrated by Archbishop Abbott in 1616. Edward Alleyn, the Shakespearean actor and founder of the College, was buried here in 1626. Several more Alleyns and Allens, warders and masters of Dulwich College, are buried in the chapel.

Richard Dowell (d.1816), organist, is buried on the north side of the communion table about six feet deep on top of the coffin of the Revd William Swanne (d.1785). The Revd Ozias Thurston Linley (d.1831), musical director and partner in the management of the Drury Lane Theatre, was the last fellow to be buried here. *23; 49; 52*

DULWICH PICTURE GALLERY & MAUSOLEUM
Dulwich, Camberwell, Surrey
(College Road, London, SE21)
The Dulwich Picture Gallery and the Mausoleum were built between the years 1811 and 1814 to the designs of Sir John Soane (1753-1837). The picture gallery was built

to contain the collection of paintings given by Noel Desenfans to his friend Sir Francis Bourgeois who bequeathed them to Dulwich College.

The mausoleum contains the remains of Noel Desenfans (d.1807), Margaret his wife (d.1813), and Sir Francis Bourgeois RA (d.1811).

Both buildings suffered bomb damage in 1944. They were restored in 1950 and 2000. *22; 23; 34; 40; 42; 49*

EAST STREET BAPTIST CHAPEL GROUND, WALWORTH*
East Street, Walworth, Surrey
(East Street, London, SE17)

This chapel was situated at the corner of Camden Street (now Morecombe Street) and East Street. Mrs Holmes noted in 1895 that the burial ground was closed and neglected and just one gravestone remained.

In 1936 workmen digging in East Street uncovered several coffins containing human remains.

The congregation now meets at the Richmond Street Baptist Mission built in 1896. *43*

EBENEZER BAPTIST CHAPEL BURIAL GROUND, BERMONDSEY
(see NECKINGER ROAD CHAPEL BURIAL GROUND, BERMONDSEY)

EWER STREET BURIAL GROUND, SOUTHWARK*
Ewer Street, Southwark Park, Surrey
(Ewer Street, London, SE1)

This small burial ground adjoined the Old Park Quaker Meeting House in Ewer Street. By 1839 the disused burial ground was in private hands. It disappeared in the 1860s when the railway was built.

In June 1987 the unidentified remains of over 200 men, women and children, presumably the remains of those people laid to rest in the old burial ground, were uncovered by workmen excavating beneath a derelict railway arch in Ewer Street. The bodies were discovered less than two feet below the surface of the ground. British Rail Properties, the owners and developers of the site, had to obtain a Home Office Licence in order to clear the ground.

The human remains were removed from the site and taken to a cemetery in East London. *17; 43*

FLEMISH BURIAL GROUND, HORSELYDOWN*
Carter Lane, Horselydown, Surrey
(Tooley street, London, SE1)

There was once a large Flemish community in Bermondsey. Their burial ground adjoined the Free Grammar School opposite St Olave's Church (qv). It was later used as an additional burial ground by the Parishes of St Olave's and St John's.

The burial ground disappeared when the approach roads to London Bridge Railway Station were laid out in the mid-19th century. *43*

FOREST HILL CEMETERY
(see CAMBERWELL CEMETERY)

GOAT'S YARD CHAPEL GROUND, HORSELYDOWN*
Goat's Yard Passage, Horselydown, Surrey
(Goat Street, London, SE1)

In 1652 a Baptist Meeting commenced at Goat's Yard, Gainsford Street, Horselydown, and in 1668 the Revd Benjamin Keach assumed the pastorate. In Mr Keach's time the meeting house was bounded by a high wall and reached by way of an avenue of limes which led to the main entrance. There was a small graveyard attached.

Mr Keach died in 1704 and was buried in Deadman's Place Burial Ground (qv). The congregation moved away about 1772, and the chapel became a cooperage and later a blacksmith's forge. Both the chapel and the graveyard have long since disappeared. *40; 58*

GUY'S HOSPITAL BURIAL GROUND, BOROUGH*
Nelson Street, Southwark, Surrey
(Snowsfields, London, SE1)

This ground was established over 400 years ago for the burial of deceased patients removed from nearby Guy's Hospital. After its closure in the 1850s it was used as a builder's yard.

In the 1890s the Vestry of Bermondsey wanted to purchase the site for a recreation ground. Guy's Hospital Medical School was built on it. *43*

GUY'S HOSPITAL CHAPEL, BOROUGH
Guy's Hospital, St Thomas' Street, Borough (St Thomas' Street, London, SE1)

Guy's Hospital Chapel is located in the centre of the west wing of the building. It was built in 1780 to the designs of Richard Jupp (1728-1799). The remains of Thomas Guy (d.1724), the founder of the hospital, rest in the crypt of the chapel. His body was removed from the vaults of St Thomas's Church (qv) in 1780. His marble tomb is by John Bacon. Also resting here are the remains of Charles Joye (d.1737), treasurer of St Thomas's and Guy's hospitals; William Hunt of Petersham (d.1829), a governor and benefactor of the hospital; and Sir Astley Paston Cooper (d.1841), surgeon to George IV. *27; 55; 57*

HANOVER CHAPEL GROUND, PECKHAM*
High Street, Peckham, Camberwell, Surrey
(Peckham High Street, London, SE15)

In 1716 a congregation of Presbyterians removed from Meeting House Lane, Peckham to a new place of worship at the corner of Rye Lane and the High Street. A small yard adjoining the chapel was used for burials.

In 1817, during the ministry of the Revd Dr W. B. Collyer (1782-1854), a new chapel was built on the same site and given the name of Hanover Chapel in recognition of its patronage by the Dukes of Kent and Sussex.

In 1848 seven coffins were removed from Hanover Chapel including those of Dr Collyer's parents and Mary his wife. They were re-interred in a new family vault at Nunhead Cemetery (qv). At the end of the 19th century the congregation removed to Bellenden Road, Peckham and in 1912 the old chapel became a cinema.

The burial ground no longer exists. *02; 23; 31*

HOLY TRINITY CHURCH, SOUTHWARK
Trinity Square, Southwark, Surrey
(Trinity Church Square, London, SE1)
The Church of Holy Trinity was built in 1823-24 to the designs of Francis Octavius Bedford (1784-1858). The masonry work was carried out by William Chadwick (1797-1852) who built several houses in Trinity Square and carried out work at St Peter's Church, Walworth (qv). William Chadwick died at Camberwell and was buried in his family vault in Nunhead Cemetery (qv). A memorial was erected in the church. Holy Trinity was built without a graveyard. The vaults beneath the church were used for interments from 1825 to 1853.

The Parish of Holy Trinity was united with the Parish of St Andrew, New Kent Road in 1956, and with St Matthew, New Kent Road in 1974. The church building was converted into the Henry Wood Concert Hall in 1975. *10; 34; 37; 43; 63*

HOLY TRINITY CHURCH, ROTHERHITHE
Rotherhithe, Surrey
(Rotherhithe Street, London, SE16)
Holy Trinity Church, Rotherhithe was built to the designs of Sampson Kempthorne (1809-73) in 1839 on land given by the Surrey Commercial Dock Company. The churchyard was in use from 1839 to 1858 when it was closed by Act of Parliament. In 1885 the churchyard was converted into a public garden by the Metropolitan Public Gardens Association, and passed to the London County Council in 1896.

The church was bombed during the blitz and many of the registers were damaged or destroyed by fire. A new church was built in 1960. The graveyard is laid out as a lawn. *10; 24; 34; 43; 44*

HONOR OAK CEMETERY
(see CAMBERWELL NEW CEMETERY)

HONOR OAK CREMATORIUM
(Brockley Way, London, SE4)
Honor Oak Crematorium was built by the Metropolitan Borough of Camberwell on land adjoining Camberwell New Cemetery (qv) in 1938-9. Five acres were laid out as a Garden of Remembrance and opened on March 29th, 1939 by the Rt Hon Lord Horder CCVO, MD, FRCP.

A columbarium was built for the reception of ashes next to the chapel. By 1987 over 97,500 bodies had been cremated here.

Notable persons cremated at Honor Oak include Professor Otakar Steinberger (d.1939), sculptor; Dr Harold Arundel Moody (d.1947), a Jamaican doctor and founder of the League of Coloured Peoples; the Revd Canon George Potter AKC (d.1960), founder of the Brotherhood of the Holy Cross and author known as 'Father Potter of Peckham'; and Beram Shapurji Saklatvala, alias Henry Marsh (d.1976), author.

Honor Oak Crematorium has been run by Southwark Council since 1965. *28*

HOOLE & MARTIN'S BURIAL GROUND, NEWINGTON *(see NEW BUNHILL FIELDS)*

KNIGHT'S BURIAL GROUND, BOROUGH*
Borough of Southwark (London, SE1)
This unidentified burial ground is twice referred to in the burial records of Nunhead Cemetery (qv), where it is recorded that in 1843 the remains of Jane Russell were deposited in a vault in the Dissenters' ground at Nunhead having been removed from Knight's Burial Ground in the Parish of St George, Southwark. In 1844 the remains of Christiana Stewart were exhumed from the same ground and were also buried at Nunhead. *02*

LOCK BURIAL GROUND, NEWINGTON*
Kent Street, Newington, Surrey
(Bricklayers Arms Roundabout, London, SE1)
The burial ground belonging to the Lock Hospital for Lepers was located some distance from the hospital. The land was given to the Parish of St George the Martyr by Robert Shawe and consecrated as a burial ground in 1712.

In 1792 James Hedger, one of the parish trustees, enclosed the burial ground by building a brick wall around it. The hospital was pulled down in 1809, and the ground was used by the Parish of St George the Martyr for the burial of paupers. It was soon overcrowded.

In 1886 the disused burial ground was laid out as St George's Recreation Ground, and most of the ground disappeared when the Bricklayers Arms flyover and roundabout was built.

The ground was cleared of all human remains between the months of October 1967 and March 1968. The unidentified remains were packed into 254 cases, and taken to Camberwell Old Cemetery (qv) where they were re-buried in nine public graves.

A portion of the former burial ground remaining after the road works had been completed was landscaped and renamed *Mayflower Gardens*. A notice in the garden states: 'Men and Women of Southwark sailed in the Mayflower from the Thames in 1620. Plaque erected by the Trustees of Pilgrim Fathers' Memorial Church which existed near this site until 1940.' *01; 43; 55*

LONG LANE BAPTIST BURIAL GROUND, BERMONDSEY
(see NECKINGER ROAD CHAPEL BURIAL GROUND BERMONDSEY)

LONG LANE QUAKER BURIAL GROUND, BERMONDSEY
Long Lane, Bermondsey, Surrey
(Long Lane, London, SE1)
This burial ground originally belonged to the Quakers and remained in use until 1855, although Mrs Holmes claims it was closed ten years earlier. Tombstones were not used in this burial ground. A small granite tablet on a wall bears the following inscription:

> The Six Weeks meeting of the
> Society of Friends.
> This tablet has been placed here
> by order of the said meeting.
> The burial ground purchased in
> 1697 was extensively used

Former burial ground in Long Lane, Bermondsey. (Photograph of 1989 by the author). *See pages 12 and 14.*

A rear view of the ruined Anglican Mortuary Chapel in Nunhead Cemetery.
(Photograph of 1983 by the author.) *See page 16.*

for Friends' Burials until closed
by order of the Privy Council
in 1855.
Eighth Month (August) 1895

Another tablet set into one of the boundary walls reads:

This wall being 29 feet and 3 inches in length is the property of and was built by John Savidge 1749 - 1750.

On another wall is the following inscription:

This wall was built in the year 1789 at the expense of and belongs to the Society of the People called Quakers.

Human remains removed from the Worcester Street Quaker Burial Ground (qv) were re-buried here in 1860. This ground, together the adjoining Neckinger Road Chapel Ground (qv) was laid out as a children's playground in 1895 and maintained by the Bermondsey Vestry. It appeared scruffy and vandalised when last visited by the author and friends in 1992. *43; 60*

LONDON ROAD BURIAL GROUND, BOROUGH*
(London Road, London, SE1)
This was a small burying ground adjoining an Independent Chapel on the east side of the London Road, Southwark. The chapel was demolished early in the 19th century and shops were built on the burial ground. *43*

MARTIN'S BURIAL GROUND, BOROUGH*
This unidentified burial ground is mentioned in Charles Knight's *Knight's London* Vol IV which was published in 1843. It was said to measure 295 feet by 379 feet and received 14,000 bodies in just 10 years. *47*

MAZE POND CHAPEL GROUND, BOROUGH*
Maze Pond, Southwark, Surrey
(Maze Pond, London, SE1)
Maze Pond Baptist Chapel originated at Fleur-de-Luce Court near Tooley Street. The congregation removed to Maze Pond about 1690. The Revd Edward Wallin (d.1733), was buried in the burial ground at the rear of the chapel.

Also buried in the graveyard were the Revd Abraham West (d.1739), the Revd Thomas Cramer (d.1773) who was described as 'a drawling and inanimate preacher' and the Revd Benjamin Wallin (d.1782), son-in-law of the Revd Edward Wallin. Another pastor, the Revd Isaac Mann (d.1831), was interred inside the chapel.

The chapel and the burial ground disappeared when Guy's Hospital Medical School was built. *43; 54; 61*

NECKINGER ROAD CHAPEL BURIAL GROUND, BERMONDSEY
Long lane, Bermondsey, Surrey
(Long Lane, London, SE1)
Neckinger Road Baptist Chapel was established in 1690. The congregation later united with members of the Back Street Independent Chapel and purchased a plot of land in Long Lane 'not adjoined to any meeting house or place of worship' for use as a cemetery. A burial vault for ministers was built in the centre of the ground.

The Revd John Sladen (d.1733 aged 46), who was the first minister of Back Street, and the Revd Henry Hunt (d.1815 aged 89), a popular preacher, were both interred here.

This burial ground was also known as the Ebenezer Baptist Chapel Burial Ground and adjoined Long Lane Quaker Burial Ground (qv). Both grounds became a children's playground in 1895.

In 1989 about twenty gravestones could still be seen, one of which was inscribed: 'The Family Vault of William James and Edward Peirse 1837'. *31; 43; 54*

NEWINGTON - A SINGULAR BURIAL
In 1875 men carrying out roadworks in front of the old Elephant and Castle public house at Newington found a single coffin beneath the surface of the road. The coffin contained a well preserved skeleton without hands or feet. The skull had been damaged. The unidentified remains were thought to date from around 1725. *58*

NEWINGTON BURIAL GROUND
(see ST MARY'S CHURCHYARD, NEWINGTON)

NEW BUNHILL FIELDS, NEWINGTON*
Deverell Street, Dover Road, Newington, Surrey
(Deverell Street, London, SE1)
This small burial ground less than one acre in extent, was opened in 1820 by Messrs Hoole and Martin as a private speculation. By 1838 over 10,000 bodies had been interred here, and by 1843, below a chapel in the centre of the ground, nearly 2,000 bodies were said to be heaped, not buried, mostly in decaying wooden coffins, in a space no more than 120ft long and 75ft wide. Thomas Jenner, a local clog and patten maker, officiated at funerals dressed as a minister of religion.

In 1835 gravediggers found the remains of a Roman cemetery in the burial ground.

The remains of Eliza Carr and two of her children were removed from the burial ground and re-buried at Nunhead Cemetery (qv) in 1848. In 1851 another two bodies were exhumed and re-buried at Nunhead.

In Nunhead Cemetery Dissenters' Section there is an inscription on a headstone which commemorates Mrs Davies of South Wales who died in 1847. It reads:

In memory of Jane Davies (whose maiden name was Richards) of Llanddewi, Aberarth, near Aberayon, Cardiganshire, South Wales, and who was buried in the burial ground around the chapel, Deverell Street, Dover Road, on whose stone was inscribed the following inscription:

Sacred
to the memory of
Jane Davies
who departed this life Nov 16, 1847
aged 67 years.

A devoted wife, an affectionate mother, and sincere Christian.

A corner of St George's Churchyard, St George's Way, Peckham.
(Photograph of 1989 by the author.) *See page 19.*

Head and foot stones stacked against the wall of the Church of St George the Martyr,
Borough High Street. (Photograph of 1989 by the author.) *See page 19.*

The burial ground was closed in 1853 and became 'Deverell's Timber Yard'. The chapel (presumably complete with its grisly contents) was taken over by the Wesleyan Methodists about 1860. After the Wesleyans left it was used as a saw mill until the Salvation Army took possession in 1900.

The chapel has long since disappeared and the disused burial ground is now (in 1989) covered by tennis courts and a youth centre. *43; 47; 51*

NEW GROTTO BURIAL GROUND, SOUTHWARK*
Dirty Lane, Southwark, Surrey
(Great Suffolk Street, London, SE1)

The Grotto Gardens Pleasure Ground was situated at the corner of George's Street and Dirty Lane. It was founded in 1760 by Thomas Finch and contained 'some lofty trees, evergreens and shrubs, and a spring'. Orchestral concerts and firework displays were held in the grounds.

In 1777 the site was acquired by the Parish of St Saviour. In 1780 some of the land was consecrated by the Bishop of Rochester on behalf of the Bishop of Winchester for use as a burial ground for the poor. The burial ground eventually disappeared when Southwark Bridge Road was laid out.

In 1884 the London Fire Brigade's Chief Station was built on part of the former burial ground and during excavations large quantities of human remains were found. *27; 57; 58*

NUNHEAD CEMETERY OF ALL SAINTS
Cemetery Road, Nunhead, Camberwell, Surrey
(Linden Grove, London, SE15)

The London Cemetery Company's Cemetery of All Saints, Nunhead, was laid out in 1839-40, and the larger part of the 52 acre site was consecrated by the Lord Bishop of Winchester on July 29th, 1840. The cemetery was a private concern, founded by the owners of Highgate Cemetery.

James Bunstone Bunning (1802-63) was the architect responsible for laying out the cemetery and designed the two gate lodges and the impressive cemetery entrance in the neo-classical style. Thomas Little designed chapels for Anglicans and Dissenters. Both chapels were built in the Gothic style in 1845. Unfortunately, the Dissenters' chapel was destroyed by enemy action in World War II, and the Anglican chapel is an empty shell as a result of arson.

At the end of the 19th century common or public burials outnumbered the sale of grave plots and private burials. Economic pressures compelled the cemetery company to abandon the cemetery in 1969, mainly because insufficient graves were being sold to make a profit and it had become too costly to employ staff to maintain the site. Between 1840 and 1969 well over 250,000 bodies had been buried here.

In 1975, following several years of neglect, Southwark Council took possession by means of *The Greater London Powers Act*.

In 1981 a voluntary group, known as the Friends of Nunhead Cemetery or FONC, was established in order to draw public awareness to the continuing plight of the vandalised cemetery and to campaign for it to be recognised as a valuable ecological and historic site.

In 1998 Southwark Council, in partnership with FONC, put in a successful bid to the Heritage Lottery Fund. The £1.25 million awarded for the restoration work is being spent on the replacement of the boundary railings (removed for salvage during World War II), stabilisation of the ruined Anglican chapel, and the restoration of fifty principal monuments. The work is expected to be completed in May 2001.

Many notable people from all walks of life lie buried in the cemetery including: Bobby Abel (d.1936), Surrey and England cricketer; Sir Charles Fox (d.1874), builder of the Crystal Palace; George Howell (d.1910), trades unionist; George Walter Thornbury (d.1876), author of the first two volumes of *Old & New London*, and the Great Vance (d.1888), actor and music hall entertainer.

Among the numerous interesting funerary monuments to be seen are several that are now listed Grade II including the magnificent granite tomb of John Allan and family by Matthew Noble 1867; the 33 ft tall granite cenotaph to the Scottish Martyrs 1851; the canopied neo-classical tomb of Vincent Figgins by W P Griffiths, architect, and John Mallcott, sculptor 1844; and the unusual terracotta Stearns Mausoleum by Doulton of Lambeth, erected in 1902.

The cemetery is designated a Grade II* landscape by English Heritage. *02; 35; 38; 43; 63*

NUNHEAD CEMETERY - ANGLICAN CHAPEL

The Grade II Listed Anglican chapel, now a ruined shell, was designed in the Gothic style by Thomas Little and built about 1845. The crypt contains a number of catacomb compartments or loculi reached by means of an entrance at the rear of the chapel. There are approximately 50 coffins in the crypt, mostly in compartments, although some were placed on the floor and damaged when inspected by the writer in 1972.

The first deposit took place in 1848 and the last in 1906. The remains of Sir Frederick Augustus Abel (d.1902) baronet and military chemist, and those of Lady Abel (d.1892), his wife of three years, lie here.

In 1951 four coffins removed from Nunhead's bomb-damaged Nonconformist Chapel (qv), including those of Samuel Straker, were placed on the floor of the crypt.

The chapel was last used for funeral services in 1969. Derelict and unattended it was gutted by arsonists in 1974. The chapel is currently undergoing Heritage Lottery Funded repair works in order to conserve it as an accessible historic ruin. *02; 21; 35*

NUNHEAD CEMETERY NONCONFORMIST CHAPEL*

The Nonconformist or Dissenters' Chapel was erected in the unconsecrated section of Nunhead Cemetery in 1845 and replaced an earlier temporary building. The tiny chapel was designed by Thomas Little in the Gothic style with burial vaults beneath. There were just four deposits in the vaults which included the remains of Samuel Straker (1806-74) a well-kown printer and stationer in the City of London, and his wife.

The chapel was irreparably damaged by enemy action during World War II, and the ruins were cleared away by the London Cemetery Company in the 1950s. All four lead coffins were removed from the crypt and transferred to the Anglican chapel in 1951. *02; 35*

NUNHEAD CEMETERY
EASTERN CATACOMBS*
The Eastern Catacombs were originally situated beneath a temporary Episcopal chapel and date from the opening of the cemetery in 1840. The temporary chapel was demolished when the permanent Anglican chapel was built at the head of the centre walk in 1845.

The floor of the former temporary chapel became the roof of the catacombs and was laid out as a raised lawn. Access to the catacombs was by means of an outside flight of stone steps leading down to an iron gate.

The main barrel-vaulted catacomb passage contains 144 compartments or loculi, 72 on each side arranged in groups of nine. Four of six anterooms on either side of the main passage contain human remains removed in 1867 from the crypt of the former Wren church of St Christopher-le-Stocks, and former churchyard which was cleared in 1933 to extend the Bank of England. One of the anterooms was used as a public vault, and another was sold in 1852 to William Clarke of Covent Garden for his family vault.

The Eastern Catacombs were badly desecrated by persons unknown in 1973, and the entrance was sealed by Southwark Council when that authority took possession in 1975.

The remains of Richard Edmonds (d.1855), a director of the ill-fated Deptford Pier Company and a local landowner, rest in the catacombs together with those of Commander John Jones RN (d.1862), and George Langermann (d.1874) only son of General Langermann of Chateau Provendroux, Belgium. *02; 06; 35*

NUNHEAD CEMETERY - SHAFT CATACOMBS*
Four unusual shaft catacombs were constructed by the London Cemetery Company, possibly to the designs of their architect and surveyor James Bunstone Bunning. Only two of the shafts were used for burials.

Early plans show three shaft catacombs on the eastern side of the cemetery and a fourth behind the monument to the Scottish Martyrs.

In 1975 the catacomb shaft adjoining the Eastern Catacombs (No 1 shaft) was surveyed by civil engineers. It was found to be 16 feet deep and contained spaces for 30 coffins. It was also found to be in a dangerous condition, consequently the exterior brickwork was demolished and the shaft was filled and closed. The shaft situated behind the Scottish Martyrs' Monument in the Dissenters section (No 2 shaft), was abandoned by the cemetery company and the outer works were demolished many years ago. The two unused shaft catacombs (Nos 3 & 4) were removed in the 1890s and the ground was later used for common graves.

There were seven deposits in No 1 shaft. The first was that of Augustus Rich of the Royal Naval School, Camberwell who died in 1842, and the last was that of James Rolls of Peckham Rye who died in 1872. Mr Rolls purchased four compartments for members of his family and was permitted to place a tombstone over the catacomb entrance.

No 2 shaft was used for at least one interment; that of Jesse Goody of Nunhead in 1843. *02; 35*

PECKHAM QUAKER BURIAL GROUND*
Hanover Street, Peckham, Camberwell, Surrey
(Highshore Road, London, SE15)
In 1826 the Society of Friends built a meeting house in Peckham. A small yard at the rear of the building was used for burials from 1832 to 1861. After its closure the Society of Friends obtained a large plot in Camberwell Cemetery (qv). Cremated remains, however, continued to be buried in the grounds of the meeting house until as late as 1959.

Mrs Holmes noted in 1895 that although the burial ground was no longer in use, a few small flat gravestones remained and the ground was 'most beautifully kept with neatly mown grass and a border of flowers'.

In 1963 the remains of 149 Quakers were exhumed from the disused burial ground and buried in the Quaker plot in Camberwell Old Cemetery. The Friends Meeting House was taken over by the GPO for use as a sorting office and the burial ground has since been built on.

Among the more notable Quakers whose remains were laid to rest in the Peckham burial ground were: William Cash (d.1849) corn merchant and maternal grandfather of Dame Elizabeth Cadbury, and Charles May FRS (d.1860) inventor and engineer.

The cremated remains of Dr Alfred Salter, the well-known GP and MP for Bermondsey who died in 1945, and those of his wife Ada, a Bermondsey Councillor who pre-deceased him in 1942, were buried in the centre of the ground. Their ashes, however, were not included in the list of human remains transferred to Camberwell Old Cemetery in 1963. *01; 03; 23; 43; 59*

PEPPER STREET CHAPEL GROUND, BOROUGH*
Pepper Street, Duke Street Park, Southwark, Surrey
(Borough, London SE1)
This was a small burial ground adjoining a Baptist chapel at the corner of Pepper Street, Duke Street Park. By 1895 the burial ground had been covered with houses. *43*

PRIORY HOUSE, PECKHAM
(see SYON HOUSE, PECKHAM)

REDCROSS STREET QUAKER BURIAL GROUND, BOROUGH*
Red Cross Street, Borough, Surrey
(Red Cross Way, London, SE1)
In 1762 the Society of Friends built a meeting house next to their burial ground in Red Cross Street. Burials ceased in 1794 and the entire site was acquired for the formation of Southwark Street in 1860. In 1887 the human remains were exhumed and re-buried elsewhere. Part of the burial ground became a small public garden. *43; 55*

ROMAN SEPULCHRAL REMAINS FOUND IN SOUTHWARK
Roman sepulchral remains were unearthed in Southwark throughout the nineteenth century. In 1812 a leaden coffin was discovered during excavations in the vicinity of the

A solitary headstone surrounded by rubbish in the former churchyard (detached section) of St George the Martyr, Southwark. (Photograph of 1989 by the author.) *See page 19.*

Headstone commemorating Captain John William Hullin in St James's Churchyard, Bermondsey. (Photograph of 1989 by the author.) *See page 21.*

Old Kent Road near the school for the deaf. The coffin, decorated with bead and reel patterns and figures of the goddess Minerva, contained a human skeleton. The area in which it was found is now covered by the Bricklayers Arms roundabout and flyover.

In 1814 the architect George Gwilt found Roman sepulchral remains under the yard of the Greyhound Inn, and four years later a Roman cemetery was found in Borough High Street when human bones were uncovered by workmen.

In 1819 Roman sandals and cinerary urns were discovered in Newcomen Street.

A large number of family sepulchres were found near the site of St Margaret's Church in 1832, and the remains of a funeral pile were found close to St Saviour's Church (now Southwark Cathedral) which may have been the site of a Roman temple.

In 1835, workmen digging in the New Bunhill Fields Burial Ground, Deverell Street found over twenty urns containing human remains buried six feet below the surface of the ground.

In Ewer Street in 1864 two human skeletons were uncovered lying next to a jar containing 500 Roman coins. A few years earlier a skeleton had been discovered in Park Street buried next to a jar of Roman coins, and a skeleton in armour was found nearby.

Roman remains were uncovered near St George the Martyr in 1889, and again in 1897, when cinerary urns containing human bones were found during the construction of a new road alongside the church. *27; 43; 37; 57*

ST GEORGE THE MARTYR, BOROUGH
High Street, Borough, Surrey
(Borough High Street, London, SE1)

The Church of St George the Martyr was built in 1736 to the designs of John Pace on the site of an earlier building. The body of the Revd Leonard Howard, Rector of St George the Martyr and Chaplain to Augusta, Princess Dowager of Wales, was interred beneath the altar in 1768.

In 1899 the crypt was cleared and 1,500 coffins were removed to Brookwood Cemetery (qv), where the site was marked by a large obelisk.

The church contains numerous memorials: William Law of Lambeth signs a large tablet to William Cody (1795); James Francis of Clapham signs a monument to Elizabeth Davidson (1798); James Marmaduke Rossetter signs a large wall tablet to Anthony Hall (1799); and Henry Hartley signs monuments to Susan Pigeon (1822) and William Toulmin (1826).

In 1816 the small churchyard was crowded with bodies. It was enlarged by Act of Parliament which allowed the purchase of land in Shaw's Court, Church Street and White Street. It remained in use until 1853. Among those buried in the churchyard were: Bishop Bonner (d.1569), who died in the Marshalsea Prison; Edward Cocker (d.1675), the mathematician; John Rushworth (d.1690), author of the *Historical Collection*; and Nahum Tate (d.1715), poet laureate and author of the Christmas carol 'While shepherds watched their flocks by night'.

In 1882 the gravestones were removed and the churchyard was converted into a public garden by the Rector and churchwardens. During construction work nine cases of unidentified human remains were removed from the ground adjoining White Street and taken to Nunhead Cemetery (qv).

About 50 headstones, their inscriptions mostly illegible, were placed against the north wall of the church. A pathetic inscription that is legible reads:

Sacred
to the memory of
Mrs Sarah Pyne
wife of Mr James Pyne
of this Parish
who died in childbed
the 29th Jany 1814
in the 38th year of her age.
Also six of her children
who died in infancy.

*'She was an affectionate wife
and tender mother'*

In 1903 a large section of the churchyard disappeared when Tabard Street was extended to Borough High Street. A list of inscriptions on the coffin plates found during excavations was deposited in the old Southwark Library. Burial records began in 1602. The last recorded burial took place in 1868. *02; 27; 37; 40; 43; 57; 58*

ST GEORGE THE MARTYR CHURCHYARD (DETACHED)
(Tabard Street, London, SE1)

The portion of St George's churchyard cut off by the new road in 1903 was converted into an open space and includes part of the site of the Marshalsea Prison. A section was opened to the public on 25th January 1902 by Mr Pomeroy, LCC Member for Rotherhithe.

The remnants of several headstones could be seen on the wall at the edge of the garden in the 1980s, but only one remained in 1990 surrounded by heaps of rubbish.

ST GEORGE THE MARTYR PAUPER BURIAL GROUND
(see LOCK BURIAL GROUND)

ST GEORGE'S CHURCH & CHURCHYARD, CAMBERWELL
Wells Street, Camberwell, Surrey
(Wells Way, London, SE5)

St George's Church was designed by Francis Octavius Bedford (1784-1858) and built between 1822 and 1824 on a plot of land given by John Rolls, a local landowner.

On the east wall a marble monument signed by Edgar George Papworth commemorated Alfred Tebbitt (d.1833). Another commemorated Mary Rolls (d.1840), wife of William Rolls of Marlborough Place. The Rolls family owned a burial vault in the crypt.

In 1970 the church was closed and little was done by its owners to make the place secure. The crypt was broken into and desecrated in 1972, 1977 and 1983. In 1988 local newspapers published horrific stories of young children

Headstones set against the boundary wall of St Mary Magdalen Churchyard, Bermondsey. (Photograph of 1989 by the author.) *See page* 23.

A solitary upright headstone commemorating Mrs Elizabeth Cross in the former churchyard of St Mary Newington. (Photograph of 1989 by the author.) *See page 23.*

playing among broken coffins and skeletons.

The churchyard measuring about one acre was used for burials from about 1825 to 1856.

In 1884 the Bishop of Rochester authorised the erection of a mortuary in the burial ground, and two years later the ground was converted into a public garden by the Metropolitan Public Gardens Association.

In 1989 about seventy headstones, their inscriptions mostly worn and barely legible, could be seen placed against the boundary walls. One commemorated Ellen, the widow of the late Lieut J. H. Mayor RN, who died on the 5th June 1840, aged 45 years.

In 1993 the church crypt was cleared and 134 coffins and 120 bags of unidentified human remains were removed to Nunhead Cemetery (qv) where they were buried in a mass grave. The earliest identified crypt burial was that of George Cooper who died 26th February 1825 aged 22, and the last was that of Mary Channell who died 7th June 1855 aged 75 years.

Among those identified and re-buried at Nunhead were members of several distinguished Camberwell families including Lieutenant Colonel Henry Roberts who died in 1838 aged 72; Pike Channell, master mariner and father of Sir William Fry Channell, Baron of the Exchequer, who died at Peckham in 1844 aged 69; and William Rolls of Marlborough Place, Old Kent Road, who died in 1845 aged 73.

The church was converted into residential flats in 1994 and the burial ground is now a car park.

NB: According to *A Survey of Parish Registers of the Diocese of Southwark* published 1970, burials took place from 1826 to 1905. *04; 08; 10; 18; 19; 23; 34; 43*

ST GEORGE'S ROMAN CATHOLIC CATHEDRAL, SOUTHWARK

St George's Road, Southwark, Surrey
(St George's Road, London, SE1)

The Roman Catholic Cathedral of St George was designed by Augustus Welby Pugin (1812-1852) and built between 1841 and 1848. It was badly damaged by enemy action in 1941, and rebuilt between 1953 and 1968.

The Revd Dr Thomas Doyle who was responsible for building the original church died in 1879 and was laid to rest in a vault in the cathedral. There is a monument to Archbishop Amigo who died in 1949.

A brass, now lost, commemorated the Reverend John Wheble who died in the Crimean War while attending Roman Catholic soldiers. *48; 53*

ST GILES'S CHURCH & CHURCHYARD, CAMBERWELL

Camberwell, Surrey
(Camberwell Church Street, London, SE5)

Camberwell is mentioned in the Domesday Book. The parish church, which replaced the earlier Anglo-Saxon church, was built in 1152 and was destroyed by fire in 1841. The present church is by Sir George Gilbert Scott and William Moffatt and dates from 1844.

Several important memorials were destroyed in the fire of 1841 and afterwards during rebuilding works.

Included amongst the many memorials said to be lost was one commemorating Bartholomew Scott (d.1600), who married the widow of Archbishop Cranmer, and others to Sir Edmond Bowyer (d.1681), Sheriff of Surrey and Sussex.; Sir Robert Waith (d.1685), Paymaster to the Navy and friend of Samuel Pepys; and Dr Wanostrocht (d.1812), Principal of Camberwell Academy.

Brasses which survived the fire were mounted on the south wall of the transept in the present church. Next to the door is a monument to Captain A. Nairne (d.1866), late of the Honourable East India Company.

St Giles' Churchyard was enlarged in 1717, 1803 and 1825. In 1731 the churchwardens agreed that no more land would be made available for brick graves.

By 1809 most of the gravestones were said to be in a poor condition, nevertheless, burials continued to take place in the churchyard until 1856 when it was closed by Act of Parliament and replaced by a new parish burial ground at Honor Oak. *(see Camberwell Cemetery)*.

By the end of the 19th century the disused churchyard was a neglected ruin. Part of the churchyard disappeared when the main road was widened and in 1938/39 the ground behind the church was cleared of gravestones and converted into a garden. About 200 headstones form a wall on the northern end of the garden. At the southern end, set against a wall, may be seen gravestones commemorating Sir Claude Champion De Crespigny (d.1818) and his wife Dame Mary (d.1812).

A tablet set into the east wall of the garden bears the following inscription:

> In the family vault near this spot lie the remains of Isabella, wife of the Revd Edward Craig and second daughter of Stephen Cattley Esq who died 21 Feb 1836.

Three former incumbents of St Giles' had monuments in the churchyard, namely the Revd Drs Richard Parr (d.1691) and Ichabod Tipping (d.1727), and the Revd Robert Aylmer MA (d.1769).

Others of note buried in Camberwell Churchyard include: the Revd Edward Wilson (d.1618), founder of Wilson's Grammar School; Sir Henry Manwaring (d.1653) former Lieutenant of Dover Castle; Sir Thomas Bond (d.1685), Lord of the Manor of Peckham; James Fisher (d.1722), sculptor of a life-sized statue of Earl Fitzwilliam of Marholm; Mary Wesley (d.1781), wife of the Revd John Wesley; Margaret Tittle Browning of St Kitts (d.1789), grandmother of the poet Robert Browning; Timothy Brown (d.1820), the 'notorious democrat' known as Equality Brown; Viscountess de Tagouhy (d.1835), widow of John Bezerra, Prime Minister of Portugal; and Adam Gordon (d.1839), a Deptford engineer and millwright, and a magistrate for the counties of Kent and Surrey.

The burial registers were deposited in the Greater London Record Office in 1953 and 1961 and cover the period 1557 to 1856. *10; 12; 23; 25; 43; 45*

ST JAMES'S CHURCHYARD, BERMONDSEY

Spa Road, Bermondsey, Surrey
(Thurland Road/Spa Road, London, SE16)

The Church of St James's, Bermondsey was built 1827-29 to the designs of James Savage (1779-1852) assisted by George Allen (1798-1847).

The extensive burial ground surrounding the church was enclosed by iron railings. After its closure in 1855 the burial ground was used as a communal clothes drying yard before being laid out as a public garden by the Metropolitan Public Gardens Association.

In 1990 approximately 100 headstones formed a wall around the garden and several large tombs could be seen in the grounds. An area set aside as a children's playground contained a covered slide with the inscription:

> Presented to the Borough Council for the use
> and enjoyment of the little children 1921.

Bermondsey in earlier times was an important maritime area, and many men connected with the sea and ships are buried or commemorated here. A well-preserved headstone commemorates Captain John Williams Hullin who drowned on Christmas Eve 1846 on his passage from Messina to London. Another commemorates Thomas Barrett Hubbard, son of Thomas Hubbard, a waterman and lighterman who died in 1846.

Near the entrance to the churchyard may be seen a small obelisk erected to the memory of Mrs Anne Caroline Lucey (d.1863) 'the amiable and beloved wife' of William Lucey, and fourth daughter of Captain Thomas Honor Cubitt of Yarmouth, Norfolk. William Lucey was a wealthy ship and barge owner. A much larger version of the obelisk may be seen over the Lucey family vault in Nunhead Cemetery (qv).

A plaque beneath a tree bears the following inscription:

> Tree planted by the
> South Bermondsey Brownies
> in memory of Cllr Mrs F J Melvin
> who passed away on 8th January 1965.
> Her last official function as chairman of
> the Beautification Committee was concerned
> with the planting of this tree at the base of
> which her ashes lie at rest.

The burial registers were deposited in the Greater London Record Office in 1965 and cover the period 1829 to 1879. The Parish of St James's was united to the Parish of Christ Church, Parkers Row. *10; 13; 34; 43*

ST JOHN'S BURIAL GROUND
(See BUTLER'S BURIAL GROUND)

ST JOHN'S CHURCH & CHURCHYARD, HORSELYDOWN
Fair Street, Horselydown, Surrey
(Fair Street/Tower Bridge Road, London, SE1)
This church was built between 1727 and 1733 by the master mason Samuel Tuffnell to the designs of Nicholas Hawksmoor (1661-1736) and John James (1673-1746). The church was bombed in 1940 and the foundations were used to build Nasmith House (London City Mission) in 1976.

Richard Russell (d.1784) a local eccentric was buried here. He left legacies to numerous charities including the Small Pox Hospital, and left £2,000 for a monument to be erected over his grave. Regrettably, his instructions were never carried out. The baronet, Sir Rowland Phillips-Langharne-Phillips, was buried here in 1832. Burials ceased in 1853.

The churchyard was converted into a public garden in 1882 and was maintained by St Olave's Board of Works until 1900, and afterwards by the Bermondsey Borough Council.

A 1914-18 war memorial stands in the garden which is well kept. Three surviving headstones lean against a wall, one of which bears the inscription:

> *Sacred*
> *to the Memory of*
> Hetty Etherington
> *wife of Joseph Etherington*
> of this Parish
> who departed this life 5th Feby 1842
> in her 45th year.

The burial registers were deposited in the Greater London Record Office in 1962, and cover the period 1733 to 1865. *10; 33; 34; 43; 53; 58*

ST JOHN'S EPISCOPAL CHAPEL GROUND, WALWORTH*
Penrose Street, Walworth, Surrey
(Penrose Street, London, SE17)
This burial ground was situated behind the Episcopal chapel and comprised over 6,000 square yards. The ground was closed in the 1850s, and railway lines of the London, Chatham and Dover Railway Company were carried over it on arches. The abandoned burial ground was later used as a dustcart and manure depot by the Newington Vestry.

The disused chapel was used as a studio and workshop by Thomas Ryan, a scenic artist, in the 1890s. *43*

ST MARGARET ON THE HILL, SOUTHWARK*
St Margaret's Hill, Borough, Surrey
(Borough High Street, London, SE1)
The Church of St Margaret was built before 1100. It was the Parish Church of Southwark until 1541 when it was united with St Mary Magdalene.

The churchyard was said to be so full that in the 16th century as many as four bodies were buried in one grave. In 1536 it was enlarged by the addition of some land belonging to Thomas Ouly. The site of the church was sold in 1545.

In 1832, during excavations for the construction of a sewer, part of the former churchyard was uncovered and large quantities of human remains were found six feet below the surface of the road. A monumental slab commemorating Aleyn Ferthing, six times Member of Parliament for Southwark in the 14th century, was uncovered and removed to St Saviour's Church (qv).

The Town Hall and Borough Compter (prison) was later built on the site and Town Hall Chambers now occupy the site. *14; 26; 27; 43; 46; 55; 57*

ST MARY'S CHURCH AND CHURCHYARD, NEWINGTON
Newington Butts, Surrey
(Newington Butts, London, SE1)
The Parish Church of St Mary Newington occupied the site of a Saxon church. The most important monument in the church commemorated Sir Hugh Brawne (d.1614) who enlarged the church in 1600 by the addition of a north aisle. The church in which Sir Hugh Brawne was buried was taken down in 1720 and his monument was transferred to the new church. In 1793 the church was again rebuilt and the Brawne tomb disappeared. Interments took place in the church and the churchyard which was also known as Newington Burial Ground.

The burial ground was enlarged in 1637, 1665, 1757 and 1834. Burials ceased in 1854. Among those buried here were: Thomas Middleton (d.1627) City chronologist and playwright, author of 'The Mask of Cupid'; Justice Tomas Lee (d.1687); George Powell (d.1704) King of the Gipsies, who died a wealthy man; William Allen (d.1768) a young man killed by soldiers in St George's Fields; William Davy (d.1780) sergeant-at-law and humorist; the Revd Dr Samuel Horsley (d.1806) Rector of St Mary Newington and Dean of Westminster; and Frederick Augustus Hartland (d.1852) pantomimist with Grimaldi at Sadlers Wells, who was accidentally killed when a plank of wood struck him on the head.

The Church of St Mary Newington was demolished in 1876 in order to widen the main road, and a new church was built in Kennington Park Road. The remains of 500 bodies were removed from the demolished church and placed in a special vault.

In 1876 at least thirteen bodies were removed to Nunhead Cemetery (qv), including members of the Dupere and Foot families of Newington. The remains of Dr Horsley and his wife were reburied at Thorley, Herts. During clearance work the skeleton of an unidentified man was discovered clothed in a black suit and wearing boots! The burial ground was converted into a garden in 1877, and a Gothic clock tower was erected on the site of the church by R. S. Faulconer, a former churchwarden.

Thirty headstones, their inscriptions mostly illegible, have been laid down at one edge of the open space next to Churchyard Row. A solitary upright stone commemorates Mrs Elizabeth Cross 'Late of this Parish' who died in 1806 aged 72 years. The inscription continues:

> In this cold grave my body lies at rest
> Till Christ my King shall rise it to be blest.
> This World is nothing but Heaven is all,
> Death did not hurt me by my fall.
> Tho' many frinds (sic) for me have cause to weep
> I am not dead but here asleep.
> At the great day of Judgment I shall rise
> With favor (sic) in the Bridegroom's eyes.

The remnants of several memorial tablets may be seen on a wall in a corner of the garden, one of which commemorates Henry Joseph Benjamin Callow who died in 1826 aged 41 years. An anonymous tablet is signed C. Smith, sculptor, 37 Gloucester Place, New Road.

The burial registers were deposited in the Greater London Record Office in 1953, and cover the periods from 1561 to 1576 and 1609 to 1854. *10; 14; 43; 46; 55*

ST MARY'S CHURCH & CHURCHYARD, ROTHERHITHE
Church Lane, Rotherhithe, Surrey
(St Marychurch Street, London, SE16)
The Parish Church of St Mary Rotherhithe was built in 1714-15 to the designs of John James (1673-1746) on the site of an earlier building. The tower by Launcelot Dowbiggin (1689-1759) was added 1747-48. The crypt contains about 1,700 coffins.

Rotherhithe was once an important maritime district, consequently many seafarers and other persons connected with the sea were laid to rest in the church and churchyard. Among the many memorials inside the church are those to Joseph Wade (d.1740) King's carver in HM dockyards at Deptford and Woolwich and Edward Hawks (d.1844) shipbuilder. There is a brass commemorating Peter Hills (d.1616) one of the elders of the Company of Trinity. Captain Christopher Jones, master of the *Mayflower*, was buried in the churchyard in 1622.

The churchyard is several feet above the level of the surrounding roadway. Several monuments and tombstones remain including a slate headstone erected to the memory of Eliza, wife of Richard Harlow who died in 1850. Richard Harlow was buried at Nunhead Cemetery (qv) in 1862. In the centre of what is now a children's play area is the tomb of Prince Le Boo of the Pelew Islands in the North Pacific. The young prince was brought to England by Captain Wilson of the *Antelope* and died of smallpox just six months later on 27th December 1784, aged 20.

The burial registers date from 1556 to 1870. *10; 24; 34; 43; 44; 56*

ST MARY'S ADDITIONAL BURIAL GROUND, ROTHERHITHE
Church Lane, Rotherhithe, Surrey
(St Marychurch Street, London, SE16)
This was a small burying ground of about one acre in size. It is detached from the main churchyard on the opposite side of the road.

The site was acquired by the churchwardens of St Mary's Parish in 1820 to supplement the overcrowded churchyard and was opened for burials in 1821. The corner watchouse was built at the same time and was in use as a storeroom for gardening tools in the 1980s.

Burials ceased in 1852 and the ground was later laid out and opened as a public garden.

In 1989 a few tombstones remained at the edge of the garden including an ornately carved headstone commemorating John Gast the shipwright who died in 1837. *24; 43*

ST MARY MAGDALEN CHURCH & CHURCHYARD, BERMONDSEY
Barnaby Street, Bermondsey, Surrey
(Bermondsey Street, London, SE1)
The Church of St Mary Magdalen was built in the 13th century next to the Priory Church of Bermondsey Abbey. The present church was built about 1675.

Churchyard of St Mary, Rotherhithe. (Photograph of 1989 by the author.) *See page 23.*

The additional burial ground of the Parish of St Mary Rotherhithe.
(Photograph of 1989 by the author.) *See page 23.*

The 17th century Puritan Divines Edward Elton (d.1624), and Jeremiah Whittaker (d.1654), former Rectors of Bermondsey, are buried here.

There are numerous monuments in the church; the oldest commemorates William Castles (d.1681). A monument to Beriah Drew (d.1829) Vestry Clerk for 46 years, is signed by local sculptor Abraham Staig. Another commemorates Dr Joseph Watson LL.D (d.1829), founder of the first public school for the education of deaf children. He is buried inside the church.

The churchyard was enlarged in 1783 and 1810. It includes a part of Bermondsey Abbey burial ground (qv). On the 17th May 1882 the churchyard was handed over to the Vestry of Bermondsey. It was converted into a garden and opened to the public on the 28th February 1883.

About a dozen tombs remain in the garden including a granite monument enclosed by iron railings belonging to the Chase family. In 1796 Mary Ann Chase left £100 to keep the tomb in good condition in perpetuity.

A memorial near the entrance to the church tells the curious story of Mrs Susanna Wood, wife of James Wood of the Kent Road, mathematical instrument maker. Mrs Wood died on the 16th June 1810 aged 57 'after a long and painful illness which she bore with the greatest fortitude.' 'She was tapped 97 times and had 461 gallons of water taken from her without ever lamenting her case or fearing the operation.' James Wood died 10th May 1837, at the great age of 108 years!

In 1989 a large number of headstones removed from the churchyard could be seen at one edge of the garden, partially hidden by a hedge and a fence.

The drinking water fountain commemorates James Buckingham Bevington JP (d.1892) of Neckinger Leather Mills. It was erected in 1902 by his son Colonel S B Bevington VD, JP, the first Mayor of Bermondsey.

The burial registers cover the period 1548 to 1865 and were deposited in the Greater London Record Office in 1966. *10; 30; 41; 43; 46; 55*

ST MARY MAGDALENE, PECKHAM*
St Mary's Road, Peckham, Camberwell, Surrey
(St Mary's Road, London, SE15)

St Mary Magdalene was built in 1839-41 to the designs of Robert Palmer Browne, to serve the growing population in the south eastern half of the Parish of St Giles' Camberwell (qv). It was built on a plot of land donated by local landowner William Edmonds of New Cross. The church was built without a churchyard.

According to Mrs Holmes the church was provided with burial vaults in the crypt, although they do not appear to have been used. In 1875 the crypt was used as a schoolroom.

Browne's church was destroyed by bombs in 1941 and a new church was built on the same site in the early 1960s to the designs of Potter and Hare. *29; 43*

ST MARY OVERIE, SOUTHWARK
The original Church of St Mary Overie was built by nuns AD 606. According to an old legend, the nunnery was founded by Mary, the ferryman's daughter. She is said to be buried in the church. A new church was built in 1106. St Mary Overie became St Saviour's in 1540 and replaced St Margaret's (qv) as the Parish Church. *(see Southwark Cathedral).*

ST OLAVE'S CHURCH & CHURCHYARD, HORSELYDOWN*
Horselydown, Surrey
(Tooley Street, London, SE1)

St Olave's Church was built on the bank of the River Thames in the 11th century. In 1327 the churchyard was flooded and human remains were swept into the river. Sir John Burcestre, Lord of the Manor of Maze, was buried here in 1466.

In 1736 part of the church collapsed when graves were dug too close to its foundations. The church was rebuilt in 1737-40 by Christopher Horsnaile and John Deval to the designs of Henry Flitcroft (1697-1769). Burials in the new church were forbidden.

A monumental inscription in the demolished church commemorated a suicide whose name was Munday. It read: 'Hallowed be the Sabbath and Farewell all Worldly Pelfe (riches); the week begins on Tuesday for Munday hath hang'd himself.'

The churchyard was closed in 1853 and the ground was afterwards used as a works depot by the Corporation of London.

The Parish of St Olave's was united with the Parish of St John, Horselydown in 1918, and eight years later the church was demolished to make way for the construction of Hay's Wharf Head Office. The site is now occupied by St Olaf House. The burial registers were deposited in the Greater London Record Office in 1962, and date from 1583 to 1853. *32; 34; 43; 46; 57; 58*

ST OLAVE'S ADDITIONAL BURIAL GROUND, HORSELYDOWN*
Tooley Street, Horselydown, Surrey
(Tooley Street, London, SE1)

This burial ground was leased to the Parish of St Olave's by the governors of St Olave's Grammar School in 1586 for 500 years. In 1733 the ground was used by the Parishes of St Olave's and St John's, Horselydown.

Burials ceased in 1853, and the area was laid out as a recreation ground in 1888 by St Olave's Board of Works. *43; 60*

ST OLAVE'S UNION BURIAL GROUND, HORSELYDOWN
Fair Street, Horselydown, Surrey
(Fair Street, London, SE1)

This ground adjoined St John's churchyard (qv) and was used for the burial of paupers who died in St Olave's Workhouse. It was closed in the 1850s and converted into a public recreation ground in 1888. *43*

ST PETER'S CHURCH AND CHURCHYARD, WALWORTH
Liverpool Street, Walworth, Surrey
(Liverpool Grove, London, SE17)

The Church of St Peter, Walworth was designed by Sir John Soane (1753-1837) and built 1823-25. Churchyard burials ceased in 1853, but the crypt, described by one writer as 'a grim depository of decomposing mortality',

Churchyard of St Peter's Church, Walworth. (Photograph of 1989 by the author.) *See page 25.*

Gwilt's tomb in the churchyard of St Saviour's Church, now Southwark Cathedral. (Photograph of 1989 by the author.) *See page 27.*

remained in use until about 1860. In 1894 the crypt was cleared of all human remains by Bishop's faculty and transferred to a cemetery. The churchyard was converted into a public garden at the expense of the Goldsmiths Company and opened by the Metropolitan Public Gardens Association in May 1895. The Newington Burial Board were responsible for looking after the site.

St Peter's Church was bombed in the blitz and thirty people sheltering in the crypt were killed and a further 100 were injured. The building was restored in 1953.

In 1989 a large number of headstones formed a broken down wall around the garden which appeared vandalised and generally rundown.

The burial registers were deposited in the Greater London Record Office and cover the period 1825 to 1896. *10; 27; 37; 43*

ST SAVIOUR'S ALMSHOUSE BURIAL GROUND
(see COLLEGE YARD BURIAL GROUND)

ST SAVIOUR'S CHURCH
(see SOUTHWARK CATHEDRAL)

ST THOMAS'S CHURCH, BOROUGH
St Thomas's Street, Southwark, Surrey
(St Thomas's Street, London, SE1)
This church was originally built during the reign of King John. In 1702 it was rebuilt by the Governors of St Thomas's Hospital; Thomas Cartwright the elder was the master mason responsible. The church was used both as the hospital chapel and parish church.

The founder of Guy's Hospital, Thomas Guy, was buried in a vault beneath the church in 1724. His remains were removed to Guy's Hospital Chapel (qv) in 1780.

St Thomas's was united with the Parish of St Saviour's in 1898, and the church became the Chapter House of Southwark Cathedral. The crypt was said to be 'crowded with unwholesome human remains' which were removed to a cemetery in 1899 by order of Her Majesty in Council.

The burial registers were deposited in the Greater London Records Office in 1948, and date from 1614 to 1854. *10; 27; 53; 55; 58*

ST THOMAS'S CHURCHYARD, BOROUGH*
St Thomas's Street, Southwark, Surrey
(St Thomas Street, London, SE1)
St Thomas's churchyard was detached from the church and reached by way of a narrow lane on the opposite side of the road. The burial ground belonged to St Thomas's Hospital and was afterwards used as a private garden. It is now lost in the grounds of Guy's Hospital. *43; 55; 58*

ST THOMAS'S HOSPITAL BURIAL GROUND*
St Thomas' Street, Southwark, Surrey
(St Thomas' Street, London, SE1)
St Thomas's Hospital was founded in the 13th century by the Priors of St Mary Overie. The original hospital was between Borough High Street and St Thomas' Street. The burial ground was some distance from the hospital. By 1895 part of the site had been covered by Bevington's leather warehouse, and asphalt tennis courts for the students of Guy's Hospital. *43; 55*

SAXON GRAVES IN BERMONDSEY*
In 1780 several Saxon graves were uncovered between Long Walk and Grange Walk close to the site of Bermondsey Abbey.

SHEERS ALLEY BURIAL GROUND, BOROUGH*
Long Lane, Southwark, Surrey
(Long Lane, London, SE1)
This small burial ground adjoined a Baptist chapel in Sheer's Alley. The ground was closed in the 1850s and the chapel was pulled down. Willmott's Buildings covered the site which was later occupied by the Southwark Mortuary and Coroner's Court. *43*

SOUTHWARK CATHEDRAL, BOROUGH
The Augustian Church of St Mary Overie (qv) was surrendered to Henry VIII at the Reformation and rededicated to St Saviour. In 1877 St Saviour's was transferred from the Diocese of Winchester to Rochester, and in 1905 it became the Cathedral Church of the newly created Diocese of Southwark.

Important tombs in the cathedral include those of John Gower (d.1848) poet and friend of Chaucer; Thomas Cure (d.1588) sadler to Queen Elizabeth I; and Dr Lancelot Andrewes (d.1626) Bishop of Winchester. Walter Tyler RA signs a monument with bust to Thomas Jones (1770). Other persons of interest buried here include: Edmund, brother of William Shakespeare (d.1607); Philip Henslowe (d.1616), vestryman, manager of the Globe theatre, money lender and brothel keeper; John Trehearne (d.1618), servant to Queen Elizabeth I and porter to King James I; Philip Massinger (d.1639), dramatist; and the Revd Francis Brockett MA (d.1680), schoolmaster at Dulwich College.

The church has been altered and rebuilt several times. In 1831 the antiquary Edward John Carlos (1798-1851) complained about the disrespectful treatment of St Saviour's dead: 'Illustrious individuals who have slept for ages in their tombs are turned unceremoniously out of their resting places like articles of timber.' He referred in particular to Bishop Andrewes and John Gower whose remains were disturbed during the rebuilding.

Burials ceased in the churchyard in 1853, however, Gwilt, the architect responsible for rebuilding the church, was interred in a special vault by authority granted by the Secretary of State in 1856. Following the ban on churchyard burials, the Burial Board of St Saviour made use of Victoria Park Cemetery in East London until the opening of Brookwood Cemetery (qv) in 1855.

The churchyard, much reduced in size, is now paved over and here and there may be seen remnants of old tombstones set into the floor of the courtyard. An inscription, barely legible, commemorates John Westmacott Eedes who died in 1841. The burial registers were deposited in the Greater London Record Office in 1952 and cover the period 1538 to 1854. *10; 43, 57*

SOUTHWARK CHAPEL BURIAL GROUND*
Chapel Place, Long Lane, Southwark
(Hankey Place, London, SE1)
Southwark Chapel was built by the Wesleyan Methodists in 1808. The adjoining graveyard was closed in the 1850s.

According to Mrs Holmes its main attraction in 1895 was a hen-coop set amongst several decaying tombstones.

The graveyard was cleared for a redevelopment scheme in 1928, and between the 15th May and 12th July that year, 57 coffins and 22 cases of unidentified human remains were removed and re-interred at Camberwell New Cemetery (qv). *01A; 43*

SURREY CHAPEL, SOUTHWARK*
Great Surrey Street, Southwark, Surrey
(Blackfriars Road, London, SE1)
Surrey Chapel was built in 1782 for the Revd Rowland Hill, a famous Dissenting preacher. When he died in 1833 his body was interred in a special vault beneath the pulpit. On the 14th April 1881, Mr Hill's remains were exhumed and placed beneath the Lincoln Tower, Christ Church, Westminster Bridge Road.

The vacated Surrey Chapel became a factory, and in 1910 it became a centre for boxing known as 'The Ring'. Sadly, this historic building was destroyed by enemy action in 1940. Rowland Hill House now occupies the site. *31; 32; 43; 55*

SUTHERLAND CHAPEL GROUND, WALWORTH
Liverpool Street, Walworth, Surrey
(Liverpool Grove, London, SE17)
Sutherland Congregational Chapel was built in 1842 by friends of the Revd Dr Andrews of Beresford Street Chapel, Walworth. A small yard adjoining the chapel was set aside for burial purposes and was in use for about 12 years. Part of the burial ground was later occupied by a school which was enlarged in 1889.

According to Mrs Holmes a few tombstones still existed in 1895. The chapel closed in 1904 and became an electric cinema and later a store for theatre props. *37; 43*

SYON HOUSE, PECKHAM*
High Street, Peckham, Camberwell, Surrey
(Peckham High Street, London, SE15)
Syon or Priory House was the home of the Nuns of Syon during their brief stay in Peckham. An avenue of tall elm trees at the rear of the house led to a small Gothic tower beside a burial plot where several nuns were laid to rest.

The mansion and grounds were acquired by John Dalton about 1818, and by 1843 a greenhouse covered the site of the nuns' graves. Syon House and its grounds have long since disappeared and the site is now occupied by Peckham Police Station. *15*

WESLEYAN CHAPEL GROUND, PECKHAM*
Stafford Street, Peckham, Camberwell, Surrey
(Staffordshire Street, London, SE15)
In 1834 the Wesleyan Methodists built a chapel in Stafford Street, Peckham. The small burial ground (about 225 square yards) adjoined their chapel and was closed in the 1850s.

In 1864 the congregation moved to a new and larger church building in Queen's Road, Peckham. The old chapel became a schoolhouse and the disused burial ground was paved over for use as the school yard.

In the 20th century the former burial ground was used as a store yard by a pickle factory and as a car park. An undated plan shows eight named graves in the burial ground. The site has been built upon. *23; 43*

WHITE STREET CHAPEL BURIAL GROUND
(see COLLIERS RENTS BURIAL GROUND)

WORCESTER STREET QUAKER BURIAL GROUND, BOROUGH*
Worcester Street, Southwark, Surrey
(O'Meara Street, London, SE1)
This was a small burying ground opened by the Society of Friends in 1666. The level of the ground was raised in 1733 to provide space for more burials, and remained in use until 1799. The ground disappeared in 1860 when Southwark Street was laid out and the London Bridge and Charing Cross Railway was constructed over the site. The contents of the burial ground, including nine lead coffins, were exhumed and re-buried in the Long Lane Quaker Ground (qv). *43*

YORK STREET INDEPENDENT CHAPEL GROUND, WALWORTH*
York Street, Lock's Fields, Walworth, Surrey
(Browning Street, London, SE17)
When York Street Independent Chapel was built in 1790 it was called Locks Fields Chapel. It was here that the famous poet Robert Browning was baptised. A small burial ground comprising about 700 square yards was located behind the chapel. At the end of the 19th century the chapel became the centre of the Browning Social Settlement. In modern times the former chapel was used as a props store by the English Music Theatre. The building was destroyed by arsonists in December 1978.

The chest tomb of Captain James Wilson (1760-1814), commander of *The Duff*, the first missionary ship to sail to the South Seas under the auspices of the London Missionary Society, was a prominent feature in the burial ground. Captain Wilson was the son-in-law of Richard Holbert (1733-1804) a founder of the chapel. The Revd Phillip Mills (d.1796), first pastor of the chapel, and the Revd Edmund Denham (d.1800), were also buried here. The graveyard was closed in the 1850s, and was laid out as a garden in 1887.

In 1994 the burial ground was cleared for a new housing scheme and between the 2nd November and 12th December all human remains were removed to Nunhead Cemetery (qv). Of the 529 bodies exhumed only 53 were positively identified including the aforementioned Captain Wilson and Richard Holbert, and Henry Shepherd (d.1808) late Water Bailiff to the City of London. The earliest identified interment in the burial ground was that of Maude Wilson, an infant who died on the 29th April 1800, and the last was that of William Woodyer who died the 16th August 1852, aged 78. *05; 27; 31; 37; 39; 43; 54*

ZION CHAPEL GROUND, BOROUGH*
High Street, Borough, Southwark, Surrey
(Borough High Street, London, SE1)
This small burial ground was situated behind the Zion Chapel in Half Moon Yard and Mermaid Court off Borough High Street. Chapel Court Dwellings later occupied the site. *43*

Sources

Manuscript documents

01) Camberwell Old Cemetery: Burial Records 1856 -
01A) Camberwell New Cemetery: Burial Records 1927 -
02) London Cemetery Company: Nunhead Cemetery Burial Records 1840 - 1969
03) List of Exhumations from the Quaker Burial Ground, Peckham, 1963
04) List of Exhumations from the Crypt of St George's Church, Camberwell, 1993
05) List of Exhumations from the York Street Chapel Burial Ground, Walworth, 1994
06) McDowall and Partners, Consulting Engineers: Survey of the Eastern Catacombs in Nunhead Cemetery, 1976

Printed documents

07) Camberwell Vestry (Parish of St Giles) - *37th Annual Report 1892-93*, 1893
08) Camberwell Borough Council - *11th Annual Report 1910-11*, 1911
09) Camberwell Borough Council - *17th Annual Report*, 1917
10) Greater London Record Office (GLRO) - *A Survey of the Parish Registers of the Diocese of Southwark, Inner London Area*, 1978

Magazines, newspapers etc

11) Devonshire, Barry, and Lawer, Frank - Parish Plots No 3: St Saviour's Southwark, *Brookwood Cemetery Society's Magazine, Necropolis News* Vol 1, No 5, 1995
12) *Gentleman's Magazine* 1825
13) *Gentleman's Magazine* 1830
14) *Gentleman's Magazine* 1832
15) *Gentleman's Magazine* 1843
16) *Leisure Hour - Extramural Interments: Woking Cemetery*, 1856
17) *London Standard 9th June 1987*
18) *South East London Mercury 8th September 1977*
19) *South London Press 26th February 1988*
20) *South London Press 6th May 1988*
21) Woollacott, Ron - 'Brief Guide to Nunhead Cemetery' Newsletter 4 of the *Peckham Society*, Feb/Mar 1976

Books etc

22) Allport, D H - *Dulwich Village*, 2nd edition 1950
23) Blanch, William Harnett - *Ye Parish of Cam(b)erwell*, 1875
24) Boast, Mary - *The Story of Rotherhithe*, 1980
25) Boast, Mary - *St Giles: The Parish Church of Camberwell*, 1987
26) Boger, Mrs E - *Bygone Southwark*, 1895
27) Bowers, Robert W - *Sketches of Southwark Old and New*, 1902
28) Camberwell Borough Council - *Jubilee Handbook*, 1950
29) Clarke, Basil - *The Parish Churches of London*, 1966
30) Clarke, E T - *Bermondsey: Its Historic Memories and Associations*, 1902
31) Cleal, Edward E - *The Story of Congregationalism in Surrey*, 1908
32) Clunn, Harold P - *Face of London*, c1951
33) Cockayne, G E - *The Complete Baronetage*, 6 vols, 1900-09
34) Colvin, Howard - *A Biographical Dictionary of British Architects 1640-1840*, 3rd edition 1995
35) Curl, James Stevens - *Nunhead Cemetery, London*, 1977
36) Darby, William - *Dulwich Discovered*, 1966
37) Darlington, Ida - *Survey of London, St George's Fields*, Volume 25, 1955
38) Friends of Nunhead Cemetery - *Illustrated Guide to Nunhead Cemetery*, 1988
39) Fullerton, W Y - *The Church Under the Hill - Denmark Place Camberwell*, c1925
40) Gorton, John - *A General Biographical Dictionary*, new edition, 4 vols, 1851
41) Gray, Geoffrey T - *Parish Church of Saint Mary Magdalen, Bermondsey*, 1958
42) Hall, Edwin T - *Dulwich History and Romance AD 967 - 1916*, 1917
43) Holmes, Mrs Basil (Isabel) - *The London Burial Grounds*, 1896
44) Humphrey, Stephen - *The Story of Rotherhithe*, 2nd edition, 1997
45) Johnston, Philip M - *Old Camberwell: Its History and Antiquities*, 1919
46) Kent, William (ed) - *An Encyclopaedia of London*, 1937
47) Knight, Charles (editor) *London, Vol IV, Chap LXXXVI, London Burials by J Saunders*, 1843
48) Meara, David - *Victorian Memorial Brasses*, 1983
49) Mee, Arthur - *The King's England, London*, 1937, 2nd edition 1948
50) Meller, Hugh - *London Cemeteries*, 1981
51) Morley, John - *Death, Heaven and the Victorians*, 1971
52) Ormiston, T L - *Dulwich College Register 1619-1926*, 1926
53) Pevsner, Nikolaus - *The Buildings of England, South London*, 1974
54) Pike, Godfrey Holden - *The Metropolitan Tabernacle: Sketches of Nonconformity in Old Southwark*, 1870
55) Roberts Sir Howard, & Godfrey, Walter H (eds) - *Survey of London, Bankside*, Volume 22, 1950
56) Saint Mary's Church, Rotherhithe, *Leaflet* 1987
57) *Victoria History of the County of Surrey*, Vol 4, 1912
58) Walford, Edward - *Old and New London, Vol VI, Southern Suburbs*, c1897
59) Walker, Olive - *A Tour of Camberwell*, 1954
60) Weinreb, Ben, & Hibbert, Christopher - *The London Encyclopaedia*, 1983
61) White, James G - *The Churches and Chapels of Old London*, 1901
62) Woollacott, Ron - *Camberwell Old Cemetery - London's Forgotten Valhalla*, 2000
63) Woollacott, Ron - *Nunhead Notables: Some of the Interesting and Important Men and Women buried in London's Nunhead Cemetery*, 1984

About the author

Ron Woollacott has long been interested in the history and development of London and its surroundings with a particular interest in South East London, and promptly joined the Peckham Society on its formation in 1975, becoming its first vice-chairman and succeeding Bob Smyth as chairman from 1978 to 1982.

A founder member of the Friends of Nunhead Cemetery (FONC) in 1981, Ron is the present chairman of this successful international voluntary organisation and carries out research on behalf of the group, including attending to grave searches and family history enquiries from all over the world. He is also a cemetery tour guide and a member of the Nunhead Cemetery Management Board, which was set up as a result of the successful £1.25 million joint Southwark Council/FONC National Heritage Lottery Award for carrying out restoration work and improvements to the historic Nunhead Cemetery.

In 1998, Southwark Council in association with the Southwark Civic Association, presented Ron with *The Honorary Liberty of the District (former Borough) of Camberwell*.

Index

Page numbers in italics = picture.

Abbott, Archbishop 10
Abel, Robert 16
Abel, Sir Frederick Augustus 16
Aged Pilgrims Asylum, Camberwell 5
All Saints' Rotherhithe 5
Allan, John 16
Allen, George 21
Allen, William 23
Alleyn, Edward 10
Amigo, Archbishop 21
Andrews, Dr Lancelot 27
Andrews, Revd Dr 28
Angell, William 8
Antelope, The 23
Aylmer, Revd Robert 21
Back Street Chapel BG 5, 14
Bacon, John 11
Bandyleg Walk BG Southwark 5
Baptists 5, 6, 8, 10, 11, 12, 14, 17, 27
Bateman, Arthur 6
Bedford, Francis (architect) 12, 19
Berkley, James 6
Bermondsey 5, 6, 11, 12, 14, 17, 21, 22, 23, 25, 27
Bermondsey Abbey BG 5, 23, 25, 27
Bermondsey Churchyard 5, 23
Bermondsey RC BG 5
Bevington, Colonel SB 25
Bevington, James 25
Blanch, William Harnett 6
Boheme, Anthony 10
Bond, Sir Thomas 21
Bonner, Bishop 19
Borough, The 5, 8, 10, 11, 12, 14, 17, 19, 22, 27, 28
Bourgeois, Sir Francis 11
Bowyer, Sir Edmond 21
Brawne, Sir Hugh 23
Bridgett (Queen of the Gypsies) 10
Brockett, Revd Francis 27
Brockley Way 6, 12
Brookwood Cemetery, Woking 5, 8, 10, 19, 27
Brown, Timothy 21
Browne, Robert P (architect) 25
Browning, Margaret Tittle 21
Browning, Robert 28
Bunning, James (architect) 16, 17
Burcestre, Sir John 25
Butler's BG Horseydown 5, 22
Cadbury, Dame Elizabeth 17
Callow, Henry 23
Camberwell (Old) Cemetery 6, 12, 17
Camberwell 5, 6, 10, 11, 12, 16, 17, 19, 21, 25, 28
Camberwell New Cemetery 6, 12, 28
Carlos, E J (antiquary) 27
Carr, Eliza 14
Carr, Revd Jonathan 10
Cartwright, Thomas 27
Cash, William 17
Castles, William 25
Cattley, Stephen 21
Chadwick, William 12
Channell, Mary & Pike 21
Channell, Sir William Fry 21
Chapel Graveyard, Boro' 6
Chase family 25
Christ Church, Rotherhithe 8
Christ Church, Southwark 5, 7, 8
Christ Church, Westminster Bridge Road 28

Christ's Hospital 6
Clarke, William 17
Cocker, Edward 19
Cody. William 19
College Yard BG Southwark 8
Colliers Rents BG Boro' 6, 8
Collyer, Mary 11
Collyer, Revd Dr Wm Bengo' 11
Congregationalists 6, 28
Cooper, George 21
Cooper, Sir Astley Paston 11
Craig, Isabella 21
Craig, Revd Edward 21
Cramer, Revd Thomas 14
Cranmer, Archbishop 21
Cross Bones BG Boro' 8, 10
Cross, Elizabeth *20*, 23
Cruden, Alexander 10
Cunningham. Peter 10
Cure, Thomas 8, 10, 27
Dalton, John 28
Davidson, Elizabeth 19
Davies, Jane 14
Davy, William 23
Dawson, James 8
Day of Camberwell (mason) 10
De Crespigny, Sir C. C. 21
De Tagouhy, Viscountess 21
Deadman's Place BG Boro' 10, 11
Denham. Revd Edmund 28
Denmark Row Baptist BG 10
Desenfans, Noel 11
Deval, John (builder) 25
Dipping Alley BG 10
Doulton of Lambeth 16
Dowbiggin, Lancelot 23
Dowell, Richard 10
Doyle, Revd Dr Thomas 21
Drew, Admiral Andrew 6
Drew, Beriah 25
Duff, The 28
Duke Street Park BG, Boro' 10
Dulwich 8, *9*, 10, 11
Dulwich BG *9*,10
Dulwich College 11, 27
Dulwich College Chapel 8, 10
Dulwich Mausoleum *9*, 10, 11
Dupere family 23
East Street Baptist Chapel BG, Walworth 11
Ebenezer Baptist Chapel BG Bermondsey 11, 14
Edmonds, Richard 17
Edmonds, William 25
Edwards, J Pasmore 8
Eedes, John Westmacott 27
Elephant & Castle 14
Elton, Rev Dr Edward 25
English Heritage 6
Etherington, Joseph & Hetty 22
Ewer Street Quaker BG 11
Faulconer, R S 23
Ferthing, Aleyn 22
Field, J D (undertaker) 8
Figgins, Vincent 16
Finch, Thomas 16
Fisher, James 21
Flemish BG, Horseydown 11
Flitcroft, Henry 25
Foot family 23
Fox, Sir Charles 16
Francis, James (stonemason)19
Friends of Nunhead Cemetery (FONC) 16, 29
Gallanhaugh, Bertram 6
Gast, John 23
George IV 11
Gloucester, Duke of 5
Goat's Yard Baptist Chapel BG, Horseydown 11
Goldsmiths Company 27

Gomm, Field Marshal Sir William Maynard 5, 8
Gomm, Lady 8
Goodman, Mrs 10
Goody, Jesse 17
Gordon, Adam 21
Gower, John 27
Gray, Robert Alexander 6
Greater London Record Office (GLRO) 21, 22, 23, 25, 27 *see note at the end of the index*
Griffiths, W P (architect) 16
Grotto Gardens 5, 16
Guy, Thomas 11, 27
Guy's Hospital 11, 14, 27
Guy's Hospital BG, Boro' 11
Guy's Hospital Chapel 11, 27
Gwilt, George (architect) 19, *26*, 27
Hall, Anthony 19
Hame, Anne and Victor 8
Hanover Chapel, Peckham 11
Harlow, Richard & Eliza 23
Hartland, Frederick Augustus 23
Hartley, Henry (stonemason) 19
Hawks, Edward 23
Hawksmoor, Nicholas (architect) 22
Hay's Wharf 25
Hedger, James 12
Henry Wood Concert Hall 12
Henslowe, Philip 27
Heritage Lottery Fund 16, 29
Hill, Revd Rowland 28
Hills, Peter 23
Hinton, Captain Thomas Eyre 8
Holbert, Richard 28
Holmes, Mrs Basil 5, 11, 12, 17, 25, 28
Holy Trinity, Rotherhithe 12
Holy Trinity, Southwark 12
Honor Oak Cemetery 6, 12
Honor Oak Crematorium 12
Hoole & Martin's BG 12, 14
Horder, Rt Hon Lord 12
Horniman, Frederick 6
Horniman's Museum 6
Horsburgh, John 10
Horseydown 5, 10, 11, 22, 25
Horsley, Revd Dr Samuel 23
Horsnaile, Christopher (builder) 25
Hough, Rt Revd Wm W 6
Howard, Revd Leonard 19
Howell, George 16
Hubbard, Thomas 22
Hullin, Captain John *18*, 22
Hunt, Revd Henry 14
Hunt, William 11
James, John 22, 23
Jenner Thomas 14
Johns, Captain Pierce 10
Jones, Christopher 23
Jones, Commander John 17
Jones, Thomas 10, 27
Joye, Charles 11
Jupp, Richard 11
Keach, Benjamin 8, 10, 11
Kempthorne, Sampson (architect) 5, 12
Kitching, General Wilfred 6
Knight's BG, Boro' 12
Langermann, George 17
Law, William (stonemason) 19
Le Boo, Prince 23
Lee, Justice 23
Lincoln Tower, Westminster Bridge Road 28
Linley, Revd Ozias 10
Little, Thomas (architect)16
Lloyd, John 8
Lock BG, Newington 12

London Cemetery Company 16, 17
London Missionary Society 28
London Necropolis Company 5
London Road BG, Boro' 14
Long Lane Baptist BG 12, *13*
Long Lane Quaker BG 12, *13*, 14, 28
Loufstone, Provost of London 5
Lucey, William and Anne 22
Mallcott, John (sculptor) 16
Mann, Revd Isaac 14
Manwaring, Sir Henry 21
Marshalsea Prison 19
Martin's BG, Boro' 14
Massinger, Philip 27
May FRS, Charles 17
Mayflower Gardens 12
Mayflower, The 12, 23
Mayor, Ellen 21
Maze Pond Baptist BG 14
Melvin, Cllr Mrs F J 22
Methodists *see* Wesleyans
Metropolitan Public Gardens Association 8, 12, 21, 22, 27
Middleton, Thomas 23
Mills, Freddie 6
Mills, Revd Phillip 28
Moffatt, William 21
Moody, Dr Harold Arundel 12
Munday (the suicide) 25
Nairne, Captain 21
Neckinger Road Chapel BG 5, 11, 14
New Bunhill Fields 12, 14, 19
New Grotto BG Southwark 5, 16
Newington 12, 14, 22, 27
Noble, Matthew (sculptor) 16
Noble, Revd John 10
Nunhead 5, 8, 11, 12, 14, 16, 17, 19, 21, 22, 23, 28
Nunhead Cemetery 5, 8, 11, 12, *13*, 14, 16, 17, 19, 21, 22, 23, 28
One Tree Hill, Honor Oak 6
Ouly, Thomas 22
Pace, John (architect) 19
Papworth, Edgar 19
Parr, Revd Dr Richard 21
Peacock, William 5
Peckham 6, 11, 12, 17, 21, 25, 28
Peckham Quaker Meeting House BG 17
Pepper Street BG, Boro' 17
Phillips-Langhame-Phillips, Sir Rowland 22
Peirse, James & Edward 14
Pigeon, Susan 19
Pike, Godfrey Holden 8, 10
Pilgrim Fathers' Memorial Church 12
Pomeroy Mr (LCC Member) 19
Potter, Revd Canon George 12
Powell, George 23
Pugin, Augustus Welby (architect) 5, 21
Pullum, William 6
Pyne, Sarah 19
Quakers 11, 12, 14, 17, 28
Redcross Street Quaker BG 17
Rich, Augustus 17
Richmond Street Mission 11
Roberts, Lt Col Henry 21
Rochester, Bishop of 8, 16, 21
Rolls, James 17
Rolls, John 19
Rolls, William & Mary 19, 21
Roman Sepulchral Remains 14, 17, 19
Rossetter, James Marmaduke (stonemason) 19
Rotherhithe 5, 8, 12, 19, 23
Rushworth. John 19
Russell, Jane 12